TRUE STORIES OF
THE REAL
MEN IN BLACK

TRUE STORIES OF
THE REAL
MEN IN BLACK

NICK REDFERN

Rosen
PUBLISHING®

New York

This edition published in 2015 by:

The Rosen Publishing Group, Inc.
29 East 21st Street
New York, NY 10010

Library of Congress Cataloging-in-Publication Data

Redfern, Nicholas, 1964- author.
True stories of the real men in black/Nick Redfern.
    pages cm.—(Off the record!)
Includes bibliographical references and index.
ISBN 978-1-4777-7837-1 (library bound)
1. Men in black (UFO phenomenon)—Juvenile literature. 2. Human-
alien encounters—Juvenile literature. 3. Unidentified flying objects—
Sightings and encounters—United States—Juvenile literature. I. Title.
BF2055.M45R434 2014
001.942—dc23
                                                        2013041894

Manufactured in the United States of America

CPSIA Compliance Information: Batch #S14YA: For further information, contact Rosen Publishing, New
York, New York, at 1-800-237-9932.

First published as *The Real Men in Black* by New Page Books/Career Press, copyright © 2011 Nick Redfern.

Metric conversions

1 inch = 2.54 centimeters; 25.4 millimeters
1 foot = 30.48 centimeters
1 yard = .914 meters
1 square foot = .093 square meters
1 square mile = 2.59 square kilometers
1 ton = .907 metric tons
1 pound = 454 grams
1 mile = 1.609 kilometers

For Brad Steiger, whose books I eagerly
devoured as a child,
and whom I am now very pleased
to call a friend.

Acknowledgments

I would like to offer my very sincere thanks to all of the following, without whom *The Real Men in Black* could never have been written:

Simon Wyatt, for his superb artistic renditions of Mothman and of the Men in Black; Rich Reynolds, of *The UFO Iconoclast*(s) blog, for truly going above and beyond the call of duty, and chasing down for me countless old, and now very hard to find, magazine articles on the Men in Black; Loren Coleman, for granting me permission to relate the story behind his own head-to-head with a Man in Black; Jim Moseley, the editor and, in his own words, "Supreme Commander" of *Saucer Smear*, for sharing with me his photographs and his many and varied memories on Albert Bender, Gray Barker, and John Keel; Brad Steiger, who very generously took valuable time out of his hectic schedule to speak at length about his tireless efforts to investigate and chronicle the activities of the MIB; my good friend and fellow author, Marie D. Jones, who enthusiastically said *Yes!* when I asked her if she would be willing to have the details of her MIB experience published in these pages; fellow researcher Regan Lee, who provided crucial data on some of the more bizarre aspects of the Men in Black mystery; Micah Hanks, for demonstrating that sometimes a Man in Black is just a man in black clothes!; Chris O'Brien, without whose fine research our knowledge of the whole Trickster phenomenon would be sorely lacking; my close friend and cohost on the *Exploring All Realms* show, Raven Meindel, for having the courage to tell her MIB-themed account of truly disturbing proportions; Irene Bott, formerly of the Staffordshire UFO Group, for the data on a 1995 Man in Black alien abduction case in central England; Daryl Collins, for an absolute treasure trove of material of decades-old correspondence and research files on Albert Bender and the MIB; Ray Boeche, without any shadow of doubt one of the most learned figures, and careful thinkers, when it comes to addressing the connections among UFOs, MIB, Christianity, demonology, and much more; Timothy Green Beckley, who kept me entertained for hours with his stories of the early years of MIB research, and who, after decades in the business, I am very pleased to say still retains his enthusiasm and passion for pursuing the Men in Black; Sharon, whose MIB confrontation in England in 1994 made me recognize that the phenomenon was very much ongoing; Allen Greenfield, for generously providing his photograph of a Man in

Black, and whose sheer depth of knowledge on the Men in Black, Gray Barker, John Keel, Tulpas, and a wide range of other issues made his words very welcome indeed; Colin Bennett, for revealing the startling facts relative to his own early-1980s encounter with a Man in Black in London, and for thoughtfully and carefully answering my many and varied questions on all manner of MIB-related issues; Joshua P. Warren, a first-class researcher and author, whose fascinating theories pertaining to the MIB and time travel provide definite food for thought; Claudia Cunningham, who was a delight to chat with, and whose recent MIB encounter is prime evidence that these dark characters are still roaming among us; Jerome Clark, who provided first-class insight and commentary on the experiences of Albert Bender and the characters of Gray Barker and John Keel that proved invaluable; Nick Pope, now retired from the British Ministry of Defense, for taking time out to give me his personal opinions and thoughts on the nature of the Men in Black controversy; Greg Bishop, without doubt one of my closest friends, and someone whose encyclopedic knowledge on the early years of and players within the UFO field made his input to the book significant in the extreme; Amanda Marino and the rest of the staff at Warwick Associates for the fine promotion and publicity work; and, finally, everyone at New Page Books and Career Press, but particularly Michael Pye, Laurie Kelly-Pye, Kirsten Dalley, Adam Schwartz, Gina Talucci, and Kara Kumpel for her fine job of editing the original manuscript of this book.

Contents

Author's Note

Throughout the pages of this book, I have used the terms *Man in Black*, *Men in Black*, and *MIB*. Whereas the first two terms are self-explanatory, the reader should note that the latter term, *MIB*, is solely used here to describe more than one such dark-suited character.

Except where otherwise noted in the text, all quotations were taken from my personal interviews with those speaking. The dates of each interview are given following the bibliography at the end of this book.

Introduction

The door banged really slowly, but hard, like someone was hitting it with his fist instead of knocking. When I opened it, there was this horrible little man about 5 feet (1.5 meters) tall. He was dressed in a black suit and tie, and had a funny little black hat on. His face was really strange; he looked like someone with anorexia, you know? His cheeks were all gaunt, his eyes were all dark, and his skin was almost white. I didn't know what to do, and just stared; it was really frightening. Then he just suddenly gave me this horrible grin, and I could tell his lips had been colored, like lipstick or something. He took off his hat and had this really bad black wig on. He looked about 60, but the wig was jet-black.

All he said was, "We would ask you cease your studies." I said, "What?" Then he repeated it, exactly the same, and I had to ask what he meant. "The sky lights; always the sky lights," he said. Then it dawned on me: I'd seen a UFO, a flying saucer thing, late at night about a week before, when my husband and I had been driving home, and we both had a really weird dream after about some little men standing around the car on the edge of the trees.

Then he said something like, "Cease and dream easy." And he gave me a really long stare like he was going to attack me or something. But he didn't; he just walked away, down the drive. I started to feel dizzy and slammed the door. I just crawled into bed and fell asleep for about three hours. But when I woke up there was this horrible smell like burning rubber all through the house. We had to have the windows open for days and get the carpets cleaned to get rid of [the smell]. It really shook me up.

The eerie statements you have just read were related to me in 1994 by a mother and housewife named Helen who to this day lives in a small, centuries-old hamlet situated within the heart of an area of central England called the Cannock Chase. During the day, the Chase is a pleasant and picturesque area of woodland. When night falls, however, it becomes a decidedly unsettling locale that reeks of hard-to-define, ethereal, and surreal foulness. And, for decades, the area and its immediate surroundings have been the dark domain of UFOs, ghosts, werewolves, Bigfoot-type beasts, and large, black, glowing-eyed cats. Helen's encounter, however, was with an entity of a nature and status that is arguably far stranger and much more ominous than any of the other anomalies could ever hope to collectively achieve (although, as will become apparent later, that very same entity may be tied in with all of the aforementioned bizarre critters). It was an entity that, within UFO and paranormal research circles, has become known as a Man in Black.

For years—or perhaps even for centuries, as I will later demonstrate—the Men in Black (MIB) have been elusive, predatory, fear-inducing figures, hovering with disturbing regularity upon the enigmatic fringes of the UFO subject, nurturing their own unique brand of terror and intimidation. Like true specters from the outer edge, the MIB appear from the murky darkness, and roam the countryside provoking carnage, chaos, paranoia, and fear in their wake, before returning to that same shrouded realm from which they originally oozed.

Very often traveling in groups of three, the MIB are a trinity of evil that seemingly appears and vanishes at will. They are often seen (in the United States) driving 1950s-style black Cadillacs and (in the British Isles) 1960s-era black Jaguars, both of which are almost always described as looking curiously brand-new. The preferred mode of dress of these sinister characters is a black suit, black fedora or homburg-style hat, black sunglasses, black necktie, black socks, black shoes, and a crisp, shining, white shirt. Very little wonder, therefore, that they have been given the name with which they are today most associated.

But who—or, far more likely, *what*—are the MIB? In the 1997 blockbuster movie *Men in Black* and its 2002 sequel, starring Hollywood celebrities Will Smith and Tommy Lee Jones, the MIB are portrayed as the secret agents of a covert arm of the U.S. government, whose role it is to hide the dark truth about the massive alien presence on the Earth. As will become undeniably clear later, however, whereas *some* MIB are indeed the secret eyes and ears of government departments, the majority of MIB appear to be of a very different breed altogether. According to certain sensational witness testimony and numerous case studies, the *real* MIB may well be alien entities themselves, carefully working to ensure that we never successfully uncover the truth about their presence, or the goal of their unearthly agenda, upon our world.

On the other hand, some students of MIB lore and legend suggest these creatures are utterly occult-based—supernatural beings that originate in, inhabit, and with disturbing regularity surface from strange and enigmatic netherworlds very different from that of our own 3D reality. A number of individuals suspect the MIB are nothing less than demons. Meanwhile, an investigator of the UFO phenomenon suggests that the Men in Black may be time travelers from humankind's far-flung future. Whatever their point—or points—of origin, however, there is one thing we can say with confidence and certainty about the Men in Black: They *are*, most assuredly, among us, and there is absolutely nothing positive or welcoming about them.

If your personal, particular area of fascination is the UFO and all its many attendant puzzles, then that trio of mysterious black-garbed men may one day be coming for you, too. If, late on some dark, thunderous, and chilled night, you are awakened from an uneasy slumber by a slow, deliberate pounding on your front door, I strongly urge you not to open it, lest you allow into your life one of the most terrifying, soulless, and macabre creatures that has ever been unleashed upon us, the human race. So, with that all now said, before you dare to proceed any further, carefully remember that you have been duly warned. Beware, always, the Men in Black...

PART I:
The Case Files

The Mystery Begins With Albert Bender (1945)

At around 3 p.m. on June 24, 1947, a pilot by the name of Kenneth Arnold was searching for an aircraft that had reportedly crashed into the southwest side of Mt. Rainier, a more than 14,000-foot (4,267 m) peak situated on Washington State's huge Cascade mountain range. His search that day was destined to discover something far different than an ordinary airplane. "I hadn't flown more than two or three minutes on my course when a bright flash reflected on my airplane," Arnold said. "It startled me, as I thought I was too close to some other aircraft. I looked every place in the sky and couldn't find where the reflection had come from until I looked to the left and the north of Mt. Rainier, where I observed a chain of nine peculiar-looking aircraft flying from north to south at approximately 9,500 feet [2,896 m] elevation and going, seemingly, in a definite direction of about 170 degrees" (Federal Bureau of Investigation 1947).

Beware of the Men in Black.

Arnold added that the mysterious craft were closing in quickly on Mt. Rainier, and he admitted to being mystified by their overall unconventional design: "I thought it was very peculiar that I couldn't find their tails, but assumed they were some type of jet plane. The more I observed these objects, the more upset I became, as I am accustomed [to] and familiar with most all objects flying whether I am close to the ground or at higher altitudes. The chain of these saucer-like objects [was] at least five miles (18 kilometers) long. I felt confident after I would land there would be some explanation of what I saw" (Federal Bureau of Investigation 1947).

So began the first-ever widely reported account of a UFO sighting in the United States. No one could offer Arnold the explanation he sought, and as the United States became a stronger magnet for strange aerial objects throughout the summer months of 1947, the military quickly swung into action, hoping to answer these vital questions: Who, exactly, was flying the saucers? Where were they from? And why were they here? It was not just the military that wanted definitive answers, either. The frenzied summer of 1947 also succeeded in firing up the minds and imaginations of everyday folk across the United States and the world, many of whom ultimately embarked upon lifelong quests to find the truth behind the saucers for themselves. Not all of them were happy with the data they unearthed, however.

In the case of a man named Albert Bender, that's putting things mildly. It was Bender, in fact, who almost singlehandedly ushered in the plague of the Men in Black—just as Arnold inaugurated the era of the UFO. For Bender, it all began with excitement and intrigue, but his story ultimately became dominated by horror, paranoia, and ill health, leaving behind a trio of cold-hearted, darkly dressed figures that have systematically mentally tortured whole swathes of the population since.

A resident of Bridgeport, Connecticut, Albert Bender had a fascination with strange and unearthly phenomena that actually predated the Kenneth Arnold affair of June 1947 by approximately a year and a half, and that ultimately spiraled downward into a full-blown, unhealthy obsession. The phenomenon that started Bender on his paranormal path occurred on December 5, 1945, when a squadron of Avenger-class aircraft vanished (under circumstances that still provoke controversy to this day) after taking to the skies from the Naval Air Station at Fort Lauderdale, Florida. The disappearance of this Flight 19, as well as a Mariner flying boat that then went in search of the ill-fated planes and their nine crew members, has today become near-legendary, and is now an integral part of the lore of the so-called Bermuda Triangle. (A far more down-to-earth theory suggests that the pilots of Flight 19 simply got lost, became catastrophically disoriented in the process, ran out of fuel, and ditched in the Atlantic, which became their final resting place.) Whatever the truth of the matter, the story immediately caught the attention of the 23-year-old Albert Bender. Using this case as a starting point, he began to dig deeply into the collective works of one of the most renowned chroniclers of all things weird and paranormal: Charles Fort, after whom the equally renowned magazine *Fortean Times* takes its name.

By the time of Kenneth Arnold's sighting in the summer of 1947, Bender was living in one of several modified sections on the top floor of an old three-story house with only his stepfather for company. As his fascination with flying saucers began to grow, Bender spent more and more time locked inside the upper room—an offshoot of the attic, in other words—where he carefully perused paranormal books, journals, and newspaper clippings, and made good use of a newly acquired telescope to, on nearly a nightly basis, excitedly scan the heavens for anything saucer-shaped.

UFOs weren't the only strange things that had gotten their hooks into Bender's mind, however. His life was steeped in the literary gothic horrors of Bram Stoker, Mary

Shelley, and Edgar Allen Poe. He also had a tremendous fascination with the occult; séances, black magic, Ouija boards, and witchcraft were all part and parcel of what it was to be Albert Bender in the late 1940s. Unsurprisingly, living a solitary existence in a dark attic (complete with the requisite creaking floorboards), Bender's character and life began to subtly change, bit by bit and piece by piece, and not in a particularly positive fashion.

One day, out of the blue, Bender took it upon himself to paint the walls of the attic with the faces of grotesque, nightmarish creatures. It was a curious task that kept him toiling busily for no less than eight months. Bender's Chamber of Horrors, as he increasingly (and justifiably) began to refer to it, was starting to take its wretched, malevolent shape. For a while at least, Bender even mused upon the idea of turning the entire upper floor into something resembling a haunted house that he planned to charge thrill-seekers to excitedly explore. Nothing ultimately came of such a venture, however, and, at a local level, Bender was beginning to develop a bit of a reputation as someone who was a tad off-kilter: By Bender's own admission, there were superstitious folk in town that had heard of his activities and viewed him as a full-blown menace.

The strange life and times of Albert Bender were blighted by psychological issues as well. He displayed clear symptoms of obsessive-compulsive disorder (OCD): He had a specific, set place for everything in his cherished attic, and he could immediately tell if anything was moved, even *slightly*, outside of its strict, rigid confines, and would become highly irritated. He was accused by friends of being overly fussy, as a result of his need to have total control over just about everything within his personal environment. Bender may also have been a full-blown hypochondriac: Although only a young man at the time his UFO interests began to develop, he lived in absolute, illogical dread of developing some form of cancer.

It should also be noted that "high strangeness" had significantly afflicted the Bender family for years prior to Albert's own experiences: A cousin of his had, as a child, undergone a nightmarish bedroom visitation from a Woman in Black—a curious (and perhaps not entirely unrelated) precursor to the nightmare in which Bender eventually found himself immersed. Another relative, in northern Pennsylvania, died of a brain hemorrhage that certain members of the family came to believe was due to the actions of a supernatural entity that haunted the shadowy corners of a nearby cemetery. In other words, for much of the Bender clan, ghosts, specters, horrific beasts, and creepy situations were central facets of everyday life. Nice.

It was in December 1950 that flying saucers took center stage for Bender. He began to more seriously collate and cross-reference the many reports and stories that came his way, he hooked up with like-minded devotees of the space people, and he embarked upon the first, tentative steps of an ambitious project: namely, to establish a worldwide network of UFO investigators to be called the International Flying Saucer Bureau (IFSB), which ultimately came to fruition in April 1952, and led Bender to publish his very own magazine, *Space Review*.

Incredibly, Bender, dwelling in the heart of a dark and shadowy occult-dominated attic in the home of his stepfather, achieved something that, I am strongly inclined to suspect, went far beyond his wildest dreams. The IFSB did not only blossom and bloom; it also caught the attention of flying saucer disciples all across the planet. UFO reports poured in to the IFSB, people eagerly clamored to become members of the group, and Bender spent night after night faithfully answering letters of the cosmic sort that reached him by the sackful.

Everything seemed to be going well: A solid network of saucer devotees had been created, the IFSB appointed representatives in a number of countries, including Britain and Australia, and, in no time at all, Bender's little group became a fairly significant force on the UFO research scene. However, in one of those classic "live fast, die young" scenarios, the IFSB—the James Dean of ufology, perhaps—was not destined to last long. It was stark fear, rather than the pompous, ego-driven bureaucracy that blights so many UFO research groups, that brought the IFSB to a grinding halt.

The beginning of the end began on the night of July 30, 1952, only a few months after the IFSB was established, when an anonymous telephone call was made to the Bender residence. With his stepfather not around, Albert was the one fate destined to answer it. When he picked up the phone, no one spoke, but Bender was instinctively certain that someone *was* at the other end of the line, listening intently in eerie silence. Bender's head suddenly spun and throbbed alarmingly, and he was forced to retire to his bed.

A few days later, fully recovered, Bender went along to his local movie theater; a new sci-fi flick was due to be screened and he was eagerly awaiting its appearance.

The movie proved to be uneventful, but the walk home, shortly before the arrival of the witching hour, was most definitely *not* uneventful. As he negotiated the dark sidewalks, an increasingly concerned Bender was sure that some hostile figure was pursuing him. He made it home without incident, however, and, as his stepfather was already sleeping, he made his quiet and careful way to the attic. On approaching the door, a fearful Bender could not fail to see that an eerie glow emanated from the thin gap directly beneath the doorframe. He flung open the door and was confronted by a strong smell of burning sulfur, and a bright, shimmering object hovering in the room. Suddenly, Bender's eyes felt severely irritated, at which point he turned on the light, and the strange object vanished into oblivion. With his OCD no doubt kicking in big-time, Bender could see that certain IFSB files were not quite where they should be; someone—or some*thing*—had been rifling through his precious flying saucer material.

Bender tried valiantly to put this unsettling experience behind him, and focused on other matters, such as the day-to-day activities of the IFSB, methodically affixing large, plastic spiders to the ceiling of the attic with which to terrify visiting friends—an entirely normal action for a 30-something, of course—and hanging out at the local cinema. The latter would, yet again, prove to be a costly action. On a dark night in November 1952, Bender was happily watching the latest science-fiction release when he was overwhelmed by a strange and unsettling feeling. It was a mixture of dread and trepidation, and a sense of being intently stared at from the darkened recesses of the old cinema.

Suddenly, out of the corner of his eye, Bender was horrified to see a human-like form materialize in a nearby seat: A well-dressed man in dark clothes had seemingly appeared out of nowhere. The shadowy figure could hardly be considered a local, however; for one thing, his eyes glowed like flashlight bulbs. Bender was once again afflicted by sudden dizziness, his head swirled, and he was forced to close his eyes as he sought to lessen the nausea that quickly threatened to engulf him. On opening them, a relieved Bender could see that the spectral being had vanished. He tried, in vain, to focus his attention on the movie again, but it was all to no avail. Minutes later, he had yet another distinct and uneasy feeling of being watched by unknown forces. Bender, slowly and apprehensively, turned around. There, yet again, was the glowing-eyed, well-dressed fiend of the night, staring coldly and harshly at Bender, who wasted no time at all in hightailing it back to the comfort of his attic.

Throughout the next few months Bender's dizzy spells continued, brief manifestations of dark-suited entities plagued his days and nights, alarming outbreaks of poltergeist activity occurred in the attic, brimstone-like odors proliferated—sometimes for days—and he began to develop intense, migraine-like headaches. It was at the height of this mental and physical torment, midway through 1953, that three men dressed in dark clothes treated Bender to the worst of all his varied visitations.

According to the initial story that quickly made the rounds in flying saucer research circles, the trio of mysterious characters revealed to a panic-stricken Bender the dark truth behind the UFO presence in our world, but warned him, in hushed but stern tones, never to reveal what he had been told—under any circumstances whatsoever. That is, unless, Bender had some sadistic wish to incur their immediate and deadly wrath, which he most certainly did not. In fact, so terrified was Bender by the whole experience that, in October 1953, he announced to his shocked followers, in the pages of his *Space Review* magazine, that he was closing the doors on the IFSB, and leaving the flying saucer arena for good.

Bender's own words on this matter, published in the final issue of the magazine, only added to the controversy: "We would like to print the full story in *Space Review*, but because of the nature of the information we are sorry that we have been advised in the negative. We advise those engaged in saucer work to please be very cautious" (Bender October 1953). And for Bender, that was that. The legend of the Men in Black, and their attendant threats, was duly born, and they had successfully claimed their first victim.

Gray Barker Joins
the IFSB
(1953)

O ne of those individuals whom Albert Bender warmly and enthusiastically invited into the IFSB fold in early 1953 was a man named Gray Barker. A resident of Clarksburg, West Virginia, Barker ran a motion-picture-booking business at the time, handling both indoor and outdoor theaters throughout his home state. Barker proved to be a highly skilled and truly atmospheric writer on all manner of flying saucer–related events and tales, and was also someone who never allowed the facts to get in the way of a good yarn. For entertainment purposes alone this was perhaps fine, but it is unfortunate when it comes to unraveling the complexities of the Bender affair, as will soon be appreciated.

Jim Moseley, a close friend of Barker's—who died in 1984—explains why Barker may have been so captivated by Albert Bender and the IFSB: "Barker's background was quite like Bender's. As a child, as an adolescent, Barker was drawn to horror movies, horror masks,

Longtime UFO investigator
Jim Moseley.

and things like that, just like Bender was. That may have had something to do with Gray wanting to get involved with the IFSB."

Barker did far more than just get involved with Bender, however. In 1956, Barker wrote and published a captivating page-turner titled *They Knew Too Much About Flying Saucers*, which devoted a considerable amount of space to the Bender controversy. Within his book, which has now achieved nearly cult status, Barker avoided *explicitly* stating that Bender's MIB were agents of the U.S. government, possibly from the FBI. That was certainly the implication that Barker made for his eager readers, however, and one that is not by any means an impossible scenario. UFO authority Jerome Clark says that it *is* likely that FBI agents visited Bender. In those dark Cold War days, Clark suggests, when nearly anybody and everybody that harbored nonconformist ideas with national-security implications—even if distant ones—found themselves under J. Edgar Hoover's bureau's gaze, "One doesn't have to speculate too hard to conclude that an active head of an early UFO organization would warrant a visit and interview. In my opinion agents may well have visited, and they may well have said something he took as threatening. From there, [Bender's] own imagination and Barker's freewheeling exploitation together generated the 'Bender mystery.'"

Clark's opinion is a valid one: In the very same year that Bender was visited by the three strange men (1953), the CIA brought together a select group called the Robertson Panel that focused much of its time and attention on the national security implications of the UFO issue. One of the more notable recommendations of the panel was that a number of the new, public UFO investigative groups in the United States at the time, such as the Civilian Saucer Investigation (CSI), and the Aerial Phenomena Research Organization (APRO), should be clandestinely watched very carefully due to "the apparent irresponsibility and the possible use of such groups for subversive purposes" (Durant 1953).

Clearly, Bender's IFSB, which quickly became a fairly significant player on the UFO scene, would also have been ripe for careful scrutiny by certain concerned elements of the U.S. intelligence community. Allen Greenfield—a ceremonial magician and a Gnostic bishop—strongly agrees. He offers his views on this issue by beginning thus: "Back in 1975, I had a meeting with Dewey Fournet, who was involved at the time of the July 1952 UFO flap over Washington, D.C. and the White House." Fournet had served in the Technical Capabilities Branch of U.S. Air Force Intelligence, until his transfer in 1952 to the Current Intelligence Branch, and became the liaison officer between the Pentagon and the Air Force's UFO investigation, Project Blue Book. The "UFO flap" to which

Greenfield refers began late on the night of July 19, 1952, and included sightings of UFOs by the military, pilots of civilian aircraft, and members of the public. It was this wave of incidents that led the FBI—after receiving a briefing on the matter from Commander Randall Boyd of the Air Force's Current Intelligence Branch—to note that "It is not entirely impossible that the objects sighted may possibly be ships from another planet such as Mars" (Federal Bureau of Investigation 1952).

The subtext that was considered far more important to the Pentagon than this sensational series of UFO sightings over D.C., states Greenfield, was that, had there been a Soviet attack on the night of the major wave of flying-saucer encounters—a first strike on the United States, in other words—then it probably would have been disastrously successful. According to what Fournet told Greenfield, because the entirety of the military apparatus was so preoccupied by looking for flying saucers—with radar and scrambled jets, as well as the sheer amount of UFO-dominated radio traffic clogging the airwaves—no meaningful attention was being given to far more conventional sources of perceived danger, like the dastardly Reds.

Greenfield spells out his personal viewpoint on this matter, which is not in accord with those of Fournet and the Air Force:

> I'm not endorsing that idea, as I think the idea of a Soviet first attack was much more mythic than the UFOs themselves. But, if you put yourself in the position of U.S. policy makers in 1952, that was a perfectly plausible scenario. And then, when the Robertson Panel was conceived, their

conclusion was that the private UFO organizations that were coming to come into existence
at that time, just like Bender's IFSB, could be
infiltrated by Communist agents and used to
set off a false UFO flap, in order to preoccupy
the entire military establishment at a vulnerable
moment, so that a sneak Soviet attack could be
successfully launched. There was the suggestion
made that it might be in the interests of national security for these private organizations to
be watched closely, or even to be closed down.
Now, not in an overt sense, as that may have
created some civil liberty issues. But, perhaps,
send someone to the door to talk to the leading
person in the organization, or to witnesses, to
scare … them, which might well have happened
with Bender.

This theory of UFO groups as national security
threats was given a further boost when, on August 28,
1953, Gray Barker himself received an ominous knock
at his front door in West Virginia. It was a special agent
of the FBI who had a whole list of questions concerning Bender's IFSB. It turns out that Bender had, some
weeks earlier, forwarded to Barker a number of business
cards that Bender had printed, identifying Barker as Chief
Investigator for the IFSB. A scared-out-of-his-wits Barker
shakily admitted to the FBI agent that he had given four
or five such cards to close friends, who still had them
when he checked in with them. It was, therefore, something of a surprise when the FBI turned up on Barker's
doorstep with one of the business cards.

The stone-faced G-man wanted to know all about the
IFSB and Barker's role within it. Ever more nervously,

Barker replied that the IFSB was simply an innocent organization formed to investigate flying saucer phenomena, and that the business cards were a means by which
investigators of the group could be identified. The FBI
man then proceeded to ask Barker if he knew a certain
individual—whose name Barker could not later recall,
no doubt as a result of being emotionally frazzled by the
interrogation—who lived in Florida. Barker replied that,
no, he did not know the man. This prompted the agent
to advise Barker that the man had suffered an epileptic
fit and had been taken to the nearby St. Mary's Hospital.
Within his belongings was an IFSB card. Satisfied that
Barker was not acquainted with the man, the FBI agent
simply thanked him for his time and departed. Barker,
meanwhile, did his very best to try and catch his breath.

After the FBI agent departed, Barker began to wonder if there really *had* been an epileptic man after all, or
if this had simply been a ruse to allow the FBI to co-
vertly check out Barker, Bender, and the IFSB. Barker
voiced all of these concerns, and several more too, in a
hastily written missive to Bender. If Barker was not lying about having been visited by a stern-faced official
of the FBI—a scenario that, given Barker's predilec-
tion for modified tales and pranks, cannot be *entirely*
ruled out, unfortunately—then this incident may have
added much weight to Barker's assertion that Bender's
three men were indeed attached to the secret world of
governmental officialdom. On a similar path, Dominic
Luchesi and August Roberts, two members of the IFSB
who subsequently became close friends of Bender, stated
that Bender's visitors were possibly from the government.
And the aforementioned Jim Moseley says that "Bender's

original story—and I met him—was that the shut-up had come from the government. It was never actually said, but maybe from the FBI."

It is highly relevant that Moseley refers to Bender's *original* story, as Bender actually told more than one version of that 1953 encounter with the three ominous men. In 1962, Barker published Bender's own, by now significantly different, tale of the event that caused him to quit flying saucer research and shut down the IFSB. It was a story told across 160 infinitely odd pages in Bender's mighty tome, *Flying Saucers and the Three Men*. In Bender's book, however, the MIB are not agents of the FBI, nor of *any* agency of the U.S. government, as Barker, back in 1956, had alluded to as a possibility in *They Knew Too Much About Flying Saucers*. In fact, they are not even of this Earth, as will now be demonstrated.

According to Albert Bender's *new*, or, perhaps, *reworked* story, on a humid night in August 1953, he was busy in the attic—where else?—hard at work on the October issue of the IFSB's monthly *Space Review* journal when a strange feeling overcame him, and the now-familiar, strong odor of brimstone saturated the room. A floorboard suddenly squeaked—which Bender immediately recognized as coming from an enclosed section of the attic adjacent to his own. Bender opened the door and, to his complete and utter terror, was confronted by the very same, glowing-eyed entity that had very nearly scared the life out of him months earlier, late on a Saturday night at the local cinema. The manifested Man in Black silently motioned Bender back into the confines of his room. He did as he was told. Bender could now see that two nearly identical figures had materialized and were following dutifully behind the first. Their clothes were black, their shoes were black, and even their homburg hats were black. All three were even wearing black gloves, as if to deliberately accentuate the unsettling MIB imagery even more. Slowly, step by step, they closed in on Bender, rather like huge spiders bearing down upon an unfortunate fly caught in some monstrous, Lovecraftian web. The three men then carefully formed a circle around Bender, and placed their hands upon his shoulders. Bender was suddenly rendered numb and passed out.

Incredibly, the tale told by Bender was that the MIB then took him from his home to—wait for it—a secret, underground installation deep below Antarctica! Indeed, in the pages of Bender's book, the locale in question sounds very much like the perfect hangout for a James Bond villain plotting to overthrow an unsuspecting world.

Bender's story—which is wholly outrageous in nature—is filled with all manner of esoteric data and quasi-scientific gobbledygook, all allegedly gleaned from the aliens as he hung out beneath the frozen wasteland. The gist of it is that those who pilot the flying saucers visit the Earth to extract an ill-defined substance from seawater that Bender theorized was almost certainly being utilized by the aliens as a power source.

After chatting genially with the cosmic visitors about their lives, cultures, religious attitudes, and more, Bender was ultimately returned to his attic, along with the following, stern warning: "You are charged to keep our secret. We do not wish to take extreme action, and you will find that you will often consider giving away some part of this information. When you get such thoughts you will be reminded of the consequences by headaches that will be almost unbearable to you. At such times beware of more serious conditions we can bring about" (Bender 1962).

The unsettling threat of the MIB could not have been made any clearer. But was there any degree of truth to Bender's—or even to Barker's—story? That is a complex question, and a tale for a later chapter; for now, it is worth noting that Bender was not the only person allegedly paid a visit by the Men in Black in 1953.

FBI Involvement (1950s)

T he same year that Bender got the visit from the Men in Black and hastily said his goodbyes to the IFSB, and Barker was grilled by the FBI, the UFO investigator Harold T. Wilkins was apprised of the facts relative to a recent, highly unusual MIB-style encounter that reportedly led the FBI to become embroiled in the strange, cosmic saga. Wilkins's source for the story insisted on anonymity, as is very often the case in such incidents, but was willing to advise Wilkins that the whole affair could be traced back to a certain official employed by a Los Angeles–based attorney's office concerned with tracing missing persons.

In a letter to Wilkins, the mysterious informant revealed that in the latter part of January 1953, two emaciated men no less than 6 ½ feet (1.98 m) in height and adorned in the now-familiar black gear arrived out of the blue at the attorney's office and were quickly and inexplicably given prestigious positions within the company, despite the fact

41

that apparently no one had any real inkling of who they were—aside from the director of the company, who chose to remain oddly tight-lipped about the situation. Whoever the strange men were, they were certainly not run-of-the-mill characters. Rather, they were weird in the extreme. Wilkins's informant advised him that the bone structures of the hands of the two men differed markedly from those normally seen in humans, such that their wrists and hands appeared to be free of joints, and one of the men possessed remarkable strength: One day, Wilkins was advised, the man in question leaned over the top of a filing cabinet, and the weight of his hand left a half-inch (1.27 centimeters) indentation in the top of the cabinet!

Not surprisingly, someone within the company chose to quickly and anonymously call in the Feds, who dispatched with high speed two G-men to investigate the curious affair. Equally unsurprisingly, with J. Edgar Hoover's finest now hot on their trail, the strange pair hot footed it to pastures unknown. That was far from being the end of the matter, however. Evidently, as Wilkins told it at least, the FBI confiscated—or in Bureau-speak, "sequestered"—the filing cabinet and turned it over to a chemist specializing in metallurgy, who determined that to produce the indentations present where one of the two men had leaned on the cabinet would have required a force of some 2,000 pounds (907 kilograms) or more. Somewhat alarmed, to say the least, the FBI, Wilkins's informant advised him, forwarded a classified report to the Bureau's Washington, D.C. headquarters, where, of course, it summarily vanished from any and all potential prying eyes.

Is there any truth to this outlandish and sensational tale? Well, here's where things get a little bit murky.

Wilkins was seemingly satisfied that his source of the story was both genuine and reliable. As were others, apparently: In abbreviated form, the case was highlighted in the August 1954 issue of *Mystic* magazine. The Men in Black were rapidly becoming the talk of the flying saucer world. A matter of mere days after the *Mystic* article appeared—which referenced the FBI's alleged involvement in the matter—a resident of Lanesville, Ohio, who had read the article, fired off a letter to J. Edgar Hoover, demanding to know the truth of the matter. In response, Hoover stated, "I would like to advise you that the article you mentioned is entirely incorrect with reference to the FBI, and there is no information on the matter which I can give you" (Federal Bureau of Investigation 1954). But Hoover was not done yet. An FBI document of August 12, 1954, states, "This article was previously brought to our attention, and the field office advised the magazine editor that the story was not true as far as the Bureau's part was concerned. The editor stated he regretted the error and he would publish a retraction in the next issue, which is not due for several months" (Federal Bureau of Investigation 1954).

Four years later, Gray Barker, Albert Bender, and the Men in Black were once again the subjects of the FBI's secret interest. On November 22, 1958, an inquiring citizen of Oklahoma City contacted J. Edgar Hoover about the FBI's treatment of UFO investigators: "Recently many rumors have been printed in UFO periodicals, concerning reports that Special Agents of the Federal Bureau of Investigation have discouraged certain saucer investigators, particularly Mr. Albert Bender of Bridgeport,

Connecticut, from further research into the secret of these elusive discs. Since you are the Director of the FBI, I would like to know whether or not these reports are factual or whether they are just rumors" (Federal Bureau of Investigation 1958).

Hoover's response was swift and to-the-point: "I am instructing a Special Agent of our Oklahoma City Office to contact you concerning the matter you mentioned." A note from Hoover to the special agent in charge at Oklahoma City added, "An agent of your office should contact [the letter writer] immediately and secure copies of or information concerning the periodicals described" (Federal Bureau of Investigation 1958). That's right: Tell the FBI, in 1950s America, that you're interested in the Men in Black, and they'll send a G-man around for a chat—no doubt an intimidating one.

In a memorandum to Hoover of December 9, 1958, the Oklahoma office of the FBI reported that the periodical in question was the *Saucerian Bulletin* published by our old friend Gray Barker. The *Bulletin* stated that the three men responsible for silencing Albert Bender were from the FBI, Air Force Intelligence, and the Central Intelligence Agency. The FBI report of December 12th reads as follows: "Bender formed the International Flying Saucer Bureau in Bridgeport, Connecticut, in 1952 to look into the flying saucer mystery. In 1953 Bender allegedly stated that he knew what the saucers are. Then 'three men in black suits' silenced Bender to the extent that even today Bender will not discuss the matter of his 'hush-up' with anyone" (Federal Bureau of Investigation 1958).

A month later, on January 22, 1959, Hoover was *still* hot on the trail of Barker and Bender—and, perhaps, even on the trail of the Men in Black, too: "The Bureau desires to obtain a copy of the book written by Gray Barker entitled *They Knew Too Much About Flying Saucers*. Reportedly, the book was published by University Books, Inc., Illinois. Contact this publishing house and if possible, obtain a copy of this book" (Federal Bureau of Investigation 1958).

Three weeks later a copy of Barker's book was, rather astonishingly, in the hands of J. Edgar Hoover, one of the most powerful and feared figures in America at the time. From the early days in that dark attic in Bridgeport, Connecticut, to the movers and shakers in Washington, D.C., Bender—and Barker—had come a very long way indeed. The FBI subsequently noted that its files contained "no information pertaining to the hush-up of Bender" (Federal Bureau of Investigation 1958). This official, internal statement specifically denying any FBI involvement in the silencing of Bender strongly seems to imply that whoever Bender's mysterious visitors were back in 1953, they were *not* agents of the FBI—a fact that might be viewed by some observers as corroboration for Bender's mind-bending *Flying Saucers and the Three Men*, in which the Men in Black have alien origins.

It is curious that *nowhere* in the now-declassified FBI papers is there any mention of the FBI's 1953 interview with Gray Barker. Can we consider this first head-to-head to have been strictly off the record in nature? Or does the FBI have its reasons for not releasing its files on the matter? Was Barker's dark-suited visitor not with the FBI, at all? Did Barker actually receive a visit from a *real* Man in Black, failing to realize the true nature of the macabre entity in his midst? Or, did Barker simply spin the story out of thin air, as a means to cruelly torture the already-stressed-out Bender?

Yet again, the mystery of the MIB proves to be as enigmatic as it does overwhelming. And, although the 1950s were about to come to an end, the Men in Black had barely gotten started.

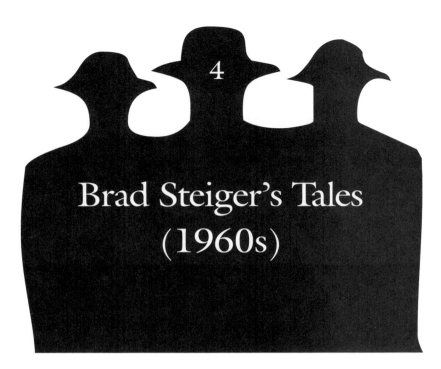

4

Brad Steiger's Tales (1960s)

Although Albert Bender birthed the MIB in the 1950s, it was in the following decade that the phenomenon really took off. One of the most learned scholars within the arena of ufology and the larger worlds of the paranormal and the supernatural is Brad Steiger, whose involvement in and keen knowledge of 1960s-era-onward MIB activity cannot be understated. Certainly, it's an integral part of the overall Men in Black history and mystery.

"When the modern saucer scene really exploded in the '40s, I was as nuts-and-bolts as anyone," Steiger said. "I think we were all secretly hoping that they, the aliens, were here; that we had made contact of some kind. Well, a few years went by, and then we're into the 1950s. And this is when I read Gray Barker's book on Albert K. Bender and his visit from the three Men in Black. My initial reaction was: Bender is saying that he has *the* answer to the UFOs? I'm thinking: *come on!* With dozens of people

47

MIB authority Brad Steiger.

trying to figure out the flying saucer mystery, *he* had the answer? But then, as I wrote more in the flying saucer field, I began corresponding with John Keel"—and that's when, in relation to the Men in Black, things really began to get moving for Steiger.

John Keel, whose real name was Alva John Kiehle, was born in 1930. As a testament to his skill as a writer even at an early age, had his very own column in a Perry, New York, newspaper by the age of 14. Drafted into the U.S. Army in 1951, Keel worked for the Armed Forces Radio Network, on one occasion even broadcasting a show from *inside* the Great Pyramid at Giza, Egypt.

Following the completion of his tour of duty with the military, Keel headed off to the Middle East for a whole series of adventures, and hung out with fakirs, magicians, and occultists, and penned a book in 1957 on these particularly memorable road-trip-style experiences: *Jadoo*. As time progressed, Keel became more and more caught up within the domain of the unknown and wrote a number of titles now considered absolute classics, including *Operation Trojan Horse*, *The Mothman Prophecies*, and *The Cosmic Question*. Keel also became one of the key, highly influential investigators of the phenomenon of the Men in Black.

Back to Brad Steiger: "In 1967, [Jim] Moseley had a big conference at the Hotel Commodore [in New York City] to celebrate 20 years of UFOs. That's where I met Tim Beckley [the author of, among numerous other titles, *Curse of the Men in Black* and *The UFO Silencers*], and we began a correspondence and a friendship that has lasted all these years. Keel was there, and many other authors in the UFO field, so all the people I had been corresponding with, I now had a chance to meet."

Steiger was finally face to face with some of the key players within the MIB research arena of the day. And, perhaps somewhat inevitably, it was not long before the man himself became immersed in the mystery of the Men in Black to a significant (and certainly unanticipated) degree. Notable reports, firsthand encounters, and even incidents involving friends began to reach Steiger—many of which were more than unsettling. Of one such report, Steiger states:

> At that time, a person who became quite a good friend of mine—a naval officer—said to me, "I

can tell you about the UFO sightings I had while I was in the service." I said, "By all means." And he told me some remarkable sightings that he had at sea and while docked in Japan—an over-flight. Then, one day, he came up to me and said, "I can't talk to you anymore; I can't associate with you." He said, "Ever since I've told you those stories, our phone rings day and night, and there's nothing but strange noises on the other end. My wife is going crazy, and she blames it on you." I said, "I'm not calling!" But she blamed the harassment on his association with me and because he knew me. I lost many friends at that time who gave me information and they would later be harassed. At the same time, there was no one knocking at my door, or no one that I could see, and there's not much that frightens me.

Steiger also had a remarkable account to relate of the most alarming elements of the saga of Albert Bender— namely, the presence of poltergeist-like phenomena in relation to a UFO experience. It was late one evening and Steiger was working in his office. Suddenly, the telephone rang. It was a call from, in Steiger's own words, an individual who is still, to this day, a well-recognized player on the UFO research scene. Steiger continued that the researcher and his fiancée had had a close sighting of a UFO, and when they returned home, violent poltergeist activity was literally tearing the place apart. As Steiger described it, he could hear screaming in the background; there were thumps and crashes, and what sounded like furniture banging together: "So, I tried to give advice and calm it. And these were techniques—metaphysical and mystical—which *did* seem to calm things down."

Unfortunately, it seems that the phenomenon behind the poltergeist activity may have become insanely enraged by Steiger's success in bringing the terrifying mayhem to a halt, for it then, immediately, set its sights on *his* home: "Right after I hung up the phone, my office just became alive with something, and there was a large crack that just appeared in the ceiling. I just said, 'Cut it out!' On another night when pictures were flying off the wall and so forth, I shouted, 'Leave me alone!' And everything stopped. And this gave me a little false confidence that maybe one could command it. Or maybe this was just a nice tactic to lure me into an even deeper situation."

Perhaps it *was* the latter, as Men in Black reports continued to pour in to Steiger HQ: "I had another friend who was with me on many of my investigations—one of the toughest guys I ever met. He was visited a number of times by decidedly weird individuals who attempted to threaten him, and on one occasion he saw them in a car and got the license plate of the vehicle they were driving. He, who was very mechanically minded, said the car they were driving didn't look like any model that he was familiar with. And he had been a private detective, and had a lot of friends on the force. He called in the license plate, and there *was* no such license plate."

And then there is the following tale from Steiger, which one would be very hard-pressed to trump: "A good friend of mine wanted to go over to Vietnam—this was when the war was going on—to visit his son, who was stationed there. He was a World War II veteran. He stopped in London first, because he had never been there and wanted to spend some time there. He wrote me quite a long letter."

The contents of the letter were decidedly odd and unsettling: Three short men of Asian appearance seemed to be shadowing Steiger's friend just about everywhere he went, around Britain's ancient capital city. "And the strangest thing," says Steiger of one experience his friend had with the three MIB, "was that he was standing at a train station, waiting to take the train to someplace, and they approached him and asked him, 'How do you get to such and such?' And he said, 'You're standing right under the sign. That's where this train goes to.' They bowed and thanked him."

This was far from the end of the story, however: When Steiger's friend got back to his hotel, he happened to look out of the window, down to the street below. To his concern he could see that there were the three men yet again, standing under a lamppost and looking directly up at the very room in which he was staying. Finally, there was a confrontation, about which the man duly wrote to Steiger. The mysterious group had approached Steiger's friend while he was on the street and said, "You are a friend of Brad Steiger, aren't you?" To which he replied, "Yes." They then made a somewhat disturbing statement: "Tell him we will visit him at Christmastime." However, there was no end-of-the-year silencing for Steiger.

Given the nature of this experience, we should not doubt Steiger's opinion when he says, "Those responsible for these types of encounters are not the Air Force; this is *not* military or paramilitary."

Mothman Arrives in Point Pleasant (1967)

S urely very few people reading this book have not at least heard of the legend of Mothman—a creature that haunted the town of Point Pleasant, West Virginia, and its surrounding areas, between November 1966 and December 1967. The diabolical exploits of the beast were chronicled in the 2002 hit Hollywood movie starring Richard Gere, *The Mothman Prophecies*, named after the book of the same title written by John Keel.

A devil-like, winged monster sporting a pair of glowing, red eyes, Mothman came hurtling into Point Pleasant out of nowhere. And, some say, its presence culminated in tragedy, doom, and death. The manifestation of Mothman also coincided with the spine-tingling appearance of more than a few of the dreaded MIB in and around Point Pleasant, too. But who, or what, was Mothman? How did the legend begin? And what was the deal with the Men in Black poking their noses into the mystery?

Mothman, the monster of Point Pleasant.

To answer those important questions, we have to go back to a dark night in November 1966, when five grave-diggers working in a cemetery in the nearby town of Clendenin were shocked to see what they described as a brown-colored, human-like, winged beast rise ominously out of the thick, surrounding trees and soar away into the distance.

Three days later, the unearthly beast surfaced once again. It was, perhaps not coincidentally, around mid-night when Roger and Linda Scarberry and Steve and Mary Mallette—two young, married couples from Point Pleasant—were passing the time by cruising around town in the Scarberrys' car. After a while, the foursome decided to head out to the dark West Virginia Ordnance Works, which was basically an abandoned explosives factory that had been used to make TNT during the Second World War, and which was situated a few miles north of Point Pleasant, in the McClintic Wildlife Station.

As they drove around the old factory, the four were puzzled to see in the shadows what looked like two red lights pointing in their direction. These were no normal lights, however. All were shocked and horrified to discover that, in reality, the lights were the glowing red eyes of a huge animal that, as Roger Scarberry later recalled, was perhaps 6 ½ or 7 feet (1.98 or 2.13 m) tall. And there were those gigantic wings, too. Not surprisingly, the couples fled the area at high speed.

Unfortunately for the Scarberrys and the Mallettes, however, the monstrous thing was far from done and seemingly decided to pursue them: As they sped off for the safety of Point Pleasant, it took to the skies and shadowed their vehicle's every movement until it reached the city limits. The four raced to the sheriff's office and told their astounding story to Deputy Millard Halstead, who later informed the media that he had known all four people for years, confirmed that none of them had criminal records, and stressed that his reason for taking their story so seriously was due to the sheer hysteria that had overwhelmed the two couples. And even though a search of the area by Halstead did not result in an answer to the mystery, Mothman was very soon to return.

Only one day after the Scarberry-Mallette encounter, Mothman decided to make an appearance for Marcella Bennett of Point Pleasant, who, around 9 p.m. on November

16th, was visiting a friend that lived close to the old TNT area. As Bennett parked and exited her vehicle, a large gray figure with red eyes seemed to rise from the very ground behind her. Such was the horror that the incident provoked in Bennett that she actually dropped her young daughter, whom she was then cradling in her arms. Scooping up the fortunately unhurt child, she raced into the home of her friend, slamming the door behind her.

And the sightings just kept on coming.

Early on the morning of November 25th, yet another remarkable encounter with the mysterious beast took place. A man named Thomas Ury was driving along Route 62 just north of Point Pleasant's TNT area when he could not fail to see a tall, gray, man-like figure standing in a field by the roadside. Suddenly, Ury later recalled, the beast opened up a large pair of wings on its back, and rose vertically into the air in a fashion that reminded Ury of a helicopter. The fear-stricken Ury added that the monster flew toward his vehicle, shadowing it with ease, even though Ury had his accelerator pedal pushed to the floor.

Throughout the next few days more and more sightings surfaced, including that of Ruth Foster of nearby Charleston, who saw the winged thing late at night in her yard, and who described it as being tall with a pair of red eyes that seemed to pop out of its face. Needless to say, the local media had an absolute field day with the mounting story of Mothman. Tales of what were referred to as "the Bird-Monster" hit the headlines, while both skeptics and local police ensured that their views and opinions on the matter were widely known. The police offered a stern warning to any and all would-be Mothman-hunters:

Keep away from the abandoned powerhouse in the TNT area after dark. Meanwhile, Dr. Robert L. Smith, associate professor of Wildlife Biology in West Virginia University's Division of Forestry, expressed his firm opinion that Mothman was nothing stranger than a large sandhill crane. This hardly satisfied the vast majority of the witnesses, however.

In the weeks and months that followed, further encounters with the bizarre beast were reported. However, they were all overshadowed by a tragic event that occurred on December 15, 1967. It was on that day that Point Pleasant's Silver Bridge—so named after its aluminum paint—that spanned the Ohio River and connected Point Pleasant to Gallipolis, Ohio, suddenly collapsed into the river, tragically claiming 46 lives. Interestingly, after the disaster at the Silver Bridge, encounters with Mothman largely came to a halt. And although a down-to-earth explanation for the bridge collapse was circulated—namely, that a fatal flaw in a single eye-bar in a suspension chain was the chief culprit—many see the cause of the disaster as being directly linked with the brooding presence of Mothman.

It was during this period—between the time when Mothman first appeared to the death and disaster on the wintery Ohio River—that the Men in Black dutifully delivered their calling cards inscribed with the words *paranoia* and *fear*. Many of those MIB cases were either chronicled by or directly involved a woman named Mary Hyre, a journalist based in Point Pleasant.

In early January 1967, Hyre, who, at the time, was working as the Point Pleasant correspondent for the Athens, West Virginia–based *Messenger* newspaper, received her own typically absurd and unsettling visit from a Man in Black. This new stranger in town wore his black hair in a bowl style, was less than 5 feet (1.5 m) in height, possessed a pair of weirdly hypnotic eyes, and had curiously thick soles on his shoes. (Notably, the late Jim Keith, who wrote his own book on the Men in Black, titled *Casebook of the Men in Black*, pointed out that "Thick shoe soles are a recurring detail in many MIB encounters" [Keith 1997].)

Crazier still, the odd little man seemed strangely entranced by Hyre's ballpoint pen. When Hyre told him he was welcome to keep it, his only response was a bone-chilling, cackle-like laugh, and he charged out of the door at high speed, vanishing into the cold, dark night as mysteriously as he had first arrived.

As she continued to delve into the puzzle of the Men in Black, UFOs, the affair of Mothman, and all its attendant oddities, Hyre began to be courted by the MIB even more, across a period of months. The strangest encounter occurred in late 1967, when a pair of Asian-appearing MIB, looking like identical twins and dressed in black overcoats, turned up at the offices of the newspaper and began making confounding conversation of the flying saucer variety.

One of the Men in Black noted, blankly, that there had recently been a lot of UFO activity in the area, a statement with which Hyre concurred. Then a barrage of questions began: Had anyone asked Hyre not to publish the details of such activity? Hyre assured the pair that, no, there had been no hush-up attempts by anyone. Then, the MIB wanted to know, what would Hyre's response be if someone *did* warn her not to print such tales? Her forthright reply was concise and clear: "I'd tell them to get lost." Perhaps this dark duo interpreted Hyre's words quite literally. After glancing back at the mounting workload on her desk for a moment, Hyre looked up again and both MIB were gone.

Clearly, there was some connection between the Men in Black and Mothman. In a later chapter, we'll meet a paranormal expert named Joshua P. Warren, who believes he may have an explanation for that mystifying connection. And a truly swirling brew of high strangeness it is, too. Until then, though, we go back to the case files.

Photographic Evidence (Late 1960s)

One of the most confounding and disturbing aspects of the Men in Black is their puzzling ability to evade capture and identification, and avoid leaving behind any physical proof of their presence. Even the U.S. Air Force, in 1967, secretly acknowledged that the MIB were seemingly always one step ahead of those who were intent on pursuing them. Evidence of this can be found in a March 1, 1967, USAF document notably titled "Impersonations of Air Force Officers" that is now in the public domain: "Information, not verifiable, has reached HQ USAF that persons claiming to represent the Air Force and other Defense establishments have contacted citizens who have sighted unidentified flying objects. In one reported case an individual in civilian clothes, who represented himself as a member of NORAD [the North American Aerospace Defense Command], demanded and received photos belonging to a private citizen. All military and civilian personnel, and particularly Information

Officers and UFO-investigating Officers who hear of such reports, should immediately notify their local OSI offices."

Clearly, even as far back as the 1960s, someone, somewhere deep within the secret world of officialdom, dearly wished to get his hands on the Men in Black and determine who they really were, from where they came, and what it was that they wanted from us. And although the document cited here was circulated extensively throughout the Air Force, it proved to be fruitless in terms of securing any meaningful results: The MIB continued to skillfully avoid even the most trained personnel of the military and the intelligence community. There are, however, a couple of (literally, just two) exceptions to this peculiar situation that stand out, and they are worthy of scrutiny. Interestingly they both date from the late 1960s, and both involve a Man in Black captured not in person, but on film.

In 1968, Timothy Green Beckley captured a Man in Black on film.

"I had my own experience with a Man in Black, when me and Jim Moseley photographed a strange individual one day back in 1968," says longtime UFO researcher and author Timothy Green Beckley, whose dogged pursuit of the MIB has persisted for decades. "There was a fellow by the name of John J. Robertson—Jack Robertson to his friends—who was the secretary for the National UFO Conference, the organization that Jim had started. Jack lived over in Jersey City. He was known as the point man as far as UFOs went on the other side of the Hudson, and had a *massive* UFO library. Jack was married to Mary. She was the psychic in the family, whereas Jack was more of a nuts-and-bolts UFO guy."

Mary was a regular user of Ouija boards, and claimed to have seen fairies in a large tree outside one of the apartment windows, and had even heard disembodied footsteps in the family home. And life was destined to get even stranger, if such a thing were possible. A fiend in black was ready to surface from the shadows, after carefully biding his time, waiting in the wings, and planning a brief reign of torment and fear. As Beckley told me, a concerned Mary informed Jack that for four days she had seen a dark-suited character in a black hat and sunglasses hunkered down in the doorway of a building next to their apartment.

Beckley states, "Mary told Jim and I he seemed to be oddly dressed, and kind of like a zombie—just standing there, very rigid. She had never engaged him in dialogues but he seemed to be surveying those going in and out of the building."

Jack Robertson later carefully placed his thoughts and recollections on record with respect to the mysterious man.

Based on his wife's description, Robertson described the Man in Black as dark and swarthy, and always possessed of a piercing, nerve-jangling expression. Robertson was a worried man. Then, as if right on cue, Beckley explains, certain other things started happening in and around the Robertson household: Strange clicking noises could be heard on the Robertsons' telephone. And, echoing the experience of Albert Bender a decade and a half earlier when his flying saucer records were thoroughly rifled, Beckley says that Robertson's precious UFO files had also been secretly scanned by someone unknown: "Jack could just tell they had been disturbed, because he had a place for everything."

Mary was becoming more and more upset by the whole situation, recalls Beckley: "She would call me up, and call Jim up, about this individual in the doorway early in the morning. Both Jim and I don't get up for anybody before noon, but Mary called so many times that Jim phoned me one day and said, 'You know, Tim, why don't we try to get up early and drive over to Jersey City, without letting Mary know that we're coming?'"

And that is precisely what the pair did. Moseley and Beckley met up, and hit the road to Jersey City with one intention: to confront the mysterious Man in Black that was torturing the mind of Mary Robertson. Beckley picks up the story again: "This was a narrow street Jack and Mary lived on, and we were following the traffic, and people were double-parked in some places. So, we're driving down the street and, sure enough, next to Mary's building, there's this guy standing, recessed into the building, like not on the sidewalk—a bit back in. He's kind of staring ahead. And he looks *just like* a Man in Black."

The Man in Black seen by Mary Robertson in 1968.

There was not a moment to lose, and it was quite literally a case of now or never. With Moseley driving and carefully keeping his eyes on the road, Beckley grabbed the camera, quickly leaned out of the window, and snapped a shot of the dark-suited stranger. As there was no place to park, unfortunately, and with the morning traffic at its height, the dynamic duo was forced to hastily pull around the corner, park the car, and then race back to the scene of all the action. Just like so many other Men in Black, unfortunately, this one had already hot footed it away from the scene. Either that or he dematerialized into the ether.

Beckley makes several important observations on the affair: "The strange thing is that after the man vanished that morning, Mary said he never appeared again. I feel, today, that Jim and I were stalking Mary's Man in Black. And I think that if that's what you do—if *you* start to get on *their* case—they vanish quickly."

For the record, it must be noted that Jim Moseley takes a *very* different stance from that of Beckley with respect to the nature of the Man in Black who appears in the photograph: "I was hoping you were going to ask me about that. I mean, truth is usually less exciting than fiction," were Moseley's opening words when I brought up the matter in conversation. Moseley's conclusion on the affair is far more down to earth than Beckley's:

> Jack was out at work, and Mary was home all day with nothing to do. And, it seems to me she started noticing somebody dressed in black, hanging around the apartment, out on the street. She became very paranoid about this— *very* paranoid. So, we drove over there, and Beckley took the photograph out of the window as we drove past the apartment. So, the picture *is* real, and there *is* a guy standing in the doorway. And, Tim *is* right: we went around the block, and when we came back the man *had* gone. The only thing that kind of made sense to me was that he was a look out … some illegal operation. But the point is, to me anyway—not to Tim, I know—it had absolutely *nothing* to do with the Robertsons or with flying saucers. He might have seen Tim taking his picture out of the car, and if he was doing something illegal that's why he left.

Regardless of whether or not Beckley and Moseley captured a genuine Man in Black on that long-gone early morning in Jersey City, even Moseley admits that within Men in Black research circles, the story and its solitary photograph have now "become a legend."

There is one more matter of relevance with respect to the saga of the Robertsons and the Men in Black: One weekend afternoon in June 1968, Jack and Mary Robertson, Jim Moseley, Gray Barker, Timothy Green Beckley, Allen Greenfield, and a variety of other ufological characters who diligently pursued the Men in Black were all seated in Cleveland, Ohio's Wild Boar Inn, enjoying drinks and lunch. What should have been a relaxing time for one and all soon changed drastically when Mary suddenly caught sight of a very pale, silver-haired man dressed in black who, with another blank-faced Man in Black, appeared to be intensely watching the group while seated at a table near the door. Mary was sure they were under secret surveillance by a pair of MIB. At that moment, the two Men in Black appeared to clearly realize they had been detected, headed quickly for the door, and disappeared into the early afternoon and oblivion.

The second case in which a Man in Black was caught on film revolves around a longtime observer and chronicler of the MIB and their actions: Allen Greenfield. Not surprisingly, when one takes into consideration its bizarre and graphic nature, Greenfield recalls the eerie encounter as if it were yesterday: "I did not mention my Men in Black experience for many years," Greenfield readily admits today, "because I'm not part of the phenomenon. I try to stay in the historian/investigator category. And if I had not been with a huge group of fellow ufologists at the time, I probably would have *never* told the story. But, there *are* other living witnesses to it."

Allen Greenfield is the author of
Secret Rituals of the Men in Black.

It was in 1969, Greenfield reveals, that he had his face-to-face encounter with a Man in Black. In keeping with what we know about the MIB, the experience was neither pleasant nor welcoming: "This was at the National UFO Conference [NUFOC], which was held that year in Charleston, West Virginia. And that would have been the June 24 weekend—which is when it was always held, because it was the date of Kenneth Arnold's sighting in 1947."

Amid the bustling throng of devotees of the UFO phenomenon, authors, researchers, members of the press, and those curious members of the public who were there just to see what all the flying saucer controversy was really about, there was someone else at the NUFOC event. It was someone strange, someone who seemed truly unearthly. It was someone with whom, by now, we have become uneasily familiar, as Greenfield notes: "There was a person there dressed in black—with dark glasses that looked almost like clip-on prescription glasses to me—who was hovering around the convention. I spotted him, but a lot of other people didn't, or they didn't pay any attention to him. Well, we took a break for lunch on the Sunday of the convention and about a dozen of us went across the street to a restaurant. And we're dining when this being began to hover around our table. He fit the classic description of the weird Men in Black: he was kind of held together very loosely, very pale and putty-like in appearance, with a mechanical-sounding voice, and stiff movements."

Greenfield decided that it was high time he confronted the darkly dressed figure, to try to determine his identity and ascertain his reason for being at the conference. After all, it's not every day that one finds oneself in the company of a Man in Black! Greenfield remembers: "At this point in time, I was very interested in the whole Walter Mitty theory for the Men in Black, that he was just some kid who's trying to freak us out, or just trying to seem important when he wasn't. But that doesn't explain the rest of it and what happened next. So, I say to him, 'Why are you following us around? What's your deal?' And I more or less leaped out of the chair, nearly knocking it over as I said it, and he immediately turned around in that robotic way that the Men in Black have. He didn't run; he walked stiffly to the door. If he was a person playing a character, he was doing it very well."

For Greenfield, however, this particular Man in Black was not about to get away—unlike most of his shadowy brethren—without Greenfield getting proof of his presence. Stressing to me that he always carried with him a state-of-the-art camera containing black-and-white, high-sensitivity, fast film, Greenfield says he raced out of the restaurant and planted himself directly in the face of the Man in Black: "I don't recall saying anything to him, except for, 'Who are you?' and he said, 'I am a Man in Black in training.' So, I said, 'Then you won't mind this,' and I quickly took a photo of him while he was frozen in place."

Captured! Allen Greenfield's Man in Black.

Greenfield was not prepared for the next startling phase of the experience, which is absolutely typical of the elusive modus operandi of the Men in Black: "The streets were essentially empty when I took the picture, which is important for what happened next. I was right by him, so I knew I had gotten the shot, but then he went around the corner, and when I got around the corner—following him—he had vanished. And I would say the amount of time involved was barely two seconds; I was right behind him, literally right behind him. I didn't expect him to be gone; I expected him to be running or walking down the street. I have no idea how to explain that, and I didn't see any place where he could have dodged into a doorway."

Greenfield could only add to me, still utterly perplexed by the surreal experience after more than 40 years: "He was gone, just gone." The priceless photograph, fortunately, remains.

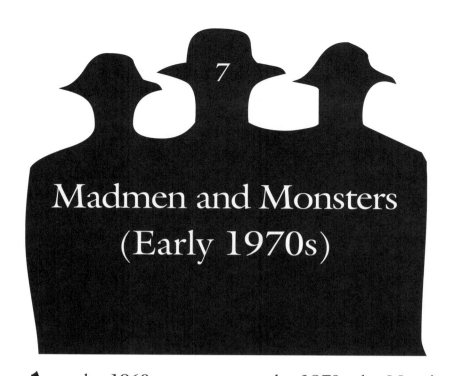

Madmen and Monsters
(Early 1970s)

A s the 1960s gave way to the 1970s the Men in Black puzzle showed no signs of being solved. In fact, for the darkly attired ones, it was pretty much business as usual. In July 1972, Patricia Hyde, a former employee of the FBI, had an encounter that brought her into direct contact with one of our mysterious, shadowy men. At around 9 o'clock on a summer's evening Hyde witnessed a strange object flying in the skies of Arcadia, Florida. Quite naturally, as is often the case following UFO encounters, Hyde wished to find out more about what she had seen. As a result, she began to dig deeper into the complexities of UFO phenomena.

Shortly after her sighting, Hyde was confronted at her apartment by an unusual-looking man dressed in dark clothing, who had deeply slanting eyes. "Miss Hyde," said the Man in Black, in a fashion that left Hyde in no doubt that his warning was a very real one, "you will stop investigating flying saucers!" Further similar visits

73

In the early 1970s, author and cryptozoologist Loren Coleman encountered a Man in Black.

occurred, and Patricia Hyde eventually got out of UFO research. Such is the effect that a traumatic encounter with a Man in Black can have on a person (Beckley 1990).

Loren Coleman, one of the world's leading cryptozoologists and the author of, among many other titles, *Bigfoot!* and, with Mark A. Hall, *True Giants*, had his own unsettling encounter in the early 1970s with a mystery man of the type that packs the pages of this book. Coleman says today of his uncanny experience: "One of the weirdest meetings I ever had with what I thought could have been a Man in Black took place when a 'Lieutenant Applegate' visited me in Decatur, Illinois" (Coleman 2010).

At the time of the visit, Coleman was looking into the strange saga of what became known as the Mad Gasser of Mattoon—a bizarre figure that, during the 1930s, terrorized the women of Botetourt County, Virginia, and, a decade later, did likewise in Mattoon, Illinois. The modus operandi of the prowler was simple: According to the legend, he chose to "gas" his unfortunate victims, render them temporarily paralyzed, and then gain access to their property—presumably to steal or take advantage of whatever or whomever caught his eye.

One of the victims of the Gasser's later attacks was a Mrs. Bert Kearney of Mattoon. On the night of September 1, 1944, around 11 p.m., Mrs. Kearney was overcome by a "sickening, sweet odor in the bedroom," that provoked a kind of creeping paralysis in her legs and burned her lips. Terrified, she screamed for her sister, Martha, who was also in the house, and breathlessly explained what was going on. Martha too could not fail to notice the strong odor. Police were quickly called, but a careful search of the property failed to find any trespasser ("Aesthetic Prowler" 1944). Later that same night, however, a mysterious man *was* seen: He was viewed lurking in the shadows outside Mrs. Kearney's bedroom window, this time by Mr. Kearney, a taxi driver who had just raced home after being alerted to the night's dramatic events. Notably, the prowler was described by Mr. Kearney as being tall, dressed entirely in black, and sporting a tight-fitting black cap. Some might suggest that the presence of a darkly dressed, sinister man in a hat, coupled with an overpowering odor that filled the bedroom and that had a negative effect on the victim, are highly reminiscent of central facets of Albert Bender's MIB experience in 1953.

Back in 1944, however, certainly no one was talking about the Men in Black. And, given that the Kearneys had what the local media described as "considerable sums of money at the house," the immediate and wholly understandable thought was that the prowler had tried to drug his victim with chloroform and then steal the cash. This was never proven, however, and as further attacks began to occur throughout the area, fear gripped the populace. Despite the fact that, throughout the years, fingers were pointed at various people suspected of being the Mad Gasser of Mattoon, the matter has never been fully resolved, and the whole series of events is still steeped in deep mystery and legend ("Aesthetic Prowler" 1944).

And it was this mystery that inadvertently led Loren Coleman to have his own encounter with a Man in Black in the early 1970s. At the time, Coleman notes, "I was looking into the mysterious Mad Gasser of Mattoon and related latter-day entities." One of those latter-day entities was Michael Hubert Kenyon, and, in December 1975, he pleaded guilty to six counts of armed robbery, and served six years in prison. Kenyon's attacks ran from the mid-1960s to the mid-1970s.

Coleman dug deeply into the exploits of the mysterious bandit that ranged from Illinois to Kansas, and Oklahoma to California: "At the time, as I often do, I was writing individual letters to many newspapers in the country, trying to track down what they had published on what I thought was a very human criminal. The pattern of similar activities that were directed to mainly women victims interested me in terms of the configuration of the Mad Gasser attacks. I wanted to make certain that any bizarre human examples that seemed to follow the random model of the Gasser be compared" (Coleman 2010).

Coleman's persistent digging into the exploits of both criminals caught someone's attention. In the midst of his research, late one night, there was a knock at the door of the Eldorado apartment in which Coleman and his first wife, Toni-Marie, were living. Coleman remembers vividly what happened next: "A darkly suited, very thin man who said he was with the

Decatur Police Department stepped into my life. He identified himself as Detective Lt. Applegate. I don't recall seeing an I.D., as those were much more trusting days. He said he was checking to see if I was the bandit, and why I was digging into this story. He said I should stop researching this series of cases. It was a startling encounter. He justified this by noting that since the bandit appeared to like media attention—he did not say how he knew this—I was targeting myself with all my letters asking for articles on the [him]. It seemed to make sense at the time" (Coleman 2010).

The next development in the story, however, most assuredly did *not* make sense. A couple of days later, Coleman checked with the DPD, a spokesperson for which stated they didn't even have a Lt. Applegate in their employ. It was then, said Coleman, that he started "wondering about whom Applegate might really have been." Coleman's final words on the matter only add to the uneasy atmosphere that permeates this story: "Years later, in doing more work on names, I discovered that 'Applegate' was another name for the devil in some literature. It was a very spooky encounter" (Coleman 2010).

Throughout the years, the MIB have played integral roles in paranormal-themed incidents that extend far beyond just UFOs, including marauding monsters like the one fabled to live in Loch Ness, a body of water formed more than 250 million years ago when massive movements in the crust of the earth led to the creation of a gigantic rift across Scotland that is now known as the Great Glen. As the centuries passed, and as the deeper parts of the Glen filled with water, the land-scape began to change, and three new, sprawling bod-ies of water were duly born: Loch Oich, Loch Lochy, and Loch Ness.

At nearly 24 miles (39 km) in length and almost a mile (1.6 km) wide, the largest of the three, Loch Ness, contains more water than any other British lake, and at its deepest point, extends to a mind-boggling depth of around 700 feet (213 m)—and possibly even deeper, some suggest. Surrounded by dense trees and ominous-looking, huge slopes, it is little wonder that Loch Ness has, for centuries, been viewed by many as both a magical and a sinister loca-tion. And as anyone who has ever marveled at the many and varied mysteries of our world will be well aware, the loch is the alleged home of Nessie—arguably the world's most famous lake monster. Or, more correctly: lake mon-sters. Beyond any doubt, if Loch Ness does harbor some-thing large and unidentified, then the possibility of there being just one creature is absurd. Only a significantly sized colony of unknown animals could be responsible for such a lengthy and ongoing phenomenon. That is, of course, if the beasts have flesh-and-blood origins—which, incredibly, may not be the case, as we will soon see.

Far stranger things have occurred at Loch Ness than mere monster sightings, such as when Aleister Crowley purchased a house on its shores in 1900. During his time at the two-century-old Boleskine House, Crowley was engaged in a magical sequence that was designed, in Crowley's words, to create a knowledge and con-versation with a guardian angel. The ritual was an elaborate one, consisting of several weeks of purifica-tion and ritual work for Crowley. At the site of what is arguably the world's most famous monster, Crowley's actions led to some highly disturbing phenomena. In his autobiography, Crowley described how the spirits he summoned at Loch Ness got wildly out of hand, causing one servant to flee and a workman to go insane. Crowley also insinuated that he was indirectly responsible for a local butcher accidentally severing an artery and dying as a consequence. Crowley had allegedly written the names of certain demons on a bill from the butcher's shop.

Richard Freeman, resident zoologist at the British-based Center for Fortean Zoology, asks, "Could it be that the demon-summoning ritual had worked in a way that Crowley had not foreseen?" Freeman continues: "Modern-day wizard Tony 'Doc' Shiels thinks this may well be the case.... Doc made the acquaintance of a man named Patrick Kelly [who] claimed to have photographed a lake monster in Lough Leane [Ireland], in 1981. This, however, was not the most fantastic of his claims" (Freeman 2005). It certainly was not: Kelly told Shiels that he was a direct descendent of Edward Kelly, the notorious scryer of Dr. John Dee, who happened to be the court magician to England's Queen Elizabeth I, and who claimed to speak with the dead via a young medium whom he had trained. The modern-day Kelly also claimed to Shiels that his father, Laurence, had met Aleister Crowley in Paris in 1933, shortly after he left the Abbey of Thelema. Crowley apparently told Laurence that he was very interested in the story of the Loch Ness Monster—whose first major flap of the 20th century was then in full swing.

The origins of the Loch Ness Monster, then, may be acutely different from what many have long presumed.

With that in mind, next in our study of the Men in Black is the case of another man who came to believe that the creatures of the loch had truly anomalous origins, and who, as a result of his investigation (or his unwise meddling, perhaps) became the target of a definitively hostile Man in Black at the loch itself.

Fredrick William Holiday was born in 1920, and was a well-known journalist, angler, cryptozoologist, and wildlife specialist. Largely prompted by sensational newspaper stories of the early 1930s, Holiday devoted much of his life to investigating the mystery of the Loch Ness Monster, and in the 1960s became a member of the Loch Ness Investigation Bureau. After several hundred hours of faithfully and carefully watching the loch, Holiday was able to claim four sightings of mysterious creatures within its deep, dark waters.

In his 1968 book, *The Great Orm of Loch Ness*, Holiday suggested that the animals might very well be monstrous invertebrates. By 1972, however, Holiday had publicly, and very radically, rejected his initial hypothesis that the Loch Ness Monsters were purely physical creatures that science had yet to classify. This can be demonstrated by his second book, *The Dragon and the Disc*. In its pages, Holiday suggested there was a definite relationship between lake monsters and UFOs. He even offered the possibility that the beasts were evil in nature, and perhaps had paranormal or demonic origins. This theory was borne out by an event that occurred on June 2, 1973. On that day, Holiday rendezvoused at Loch Ness with a Reverend Dr. Donald Omand, who was about to attempt something truly remarkable and probably unique: nothing less than a full-fledged exorcism of Loch Ness.

In Holiday's own words, "We stopped first at the beach of Lochend where a protective ceremony was enacted. This consisted of a brief service followed by the application of holy water to the foreheads of the participants." Dr. Omand then intoned, "Grant that by the power entrusted to Thy unworthy servant, this highland loch, and the land adjoining it may be delivered from all evil spirits" (Holiday 1986). The group then made its careful way, via Inverness, to the southeast shore, on to Fort Augustus, and then to the ruined remains of Urquhart Castle. At each location, an exorcism was faithfully performed. The culmination of the day's events was a cleansing ritual aboard a boat in the middle of Loch Ness itself. Holiday admitted with some degree of concern that he fully expected one of the mighty beasts of the loch to wildly break the surface of the deep waters at the height of the exorcism. Fortunately for both him and Dr. Omand, however, such a creature failed to appear.

Although many mainstream researchers and students of the monsters of Loch Ness loudly scoff at the notion that they might be anything more—or, paradoxically, anything less—than flesh-and-blood creatures, others have been prepared to at least look at the data suggesting that the paranormal might play some role in the ongoing Loch Ness controversy. One of those was a renowned Loch Ness Monster hunter named Tim Dinsdale, who, commenting on the exorcism of Dr. Omand, publicly said, "I was not inclined to scoff at Dr. Omand, or those associated with him, though I could hardly subscribe to the belief that the monster was a phantom. Having seen and filmed it I knew otherwise, but where the dark forces were concerned, if Dr. Omand believed it was possible to rid the place of them he deserved to be given a respectful hearing" (Dinsdale 1976).

Interestingly, despite his *public* statement that he could hardly accept the idea that the monster of the loch had supernatural origins, in a *private* letter to Holiday in 1974, Dinsdale wrote that he had been personally aware for some years of what seemed to be a paranormal element to the Loch Ness Monster phenomenon. Ted Holiday actually had very good reason to believe that there was something highly strange about the beasts of Loch Ness, and that all was not as it initially seemed. Commenting on his monster-hunting activities at the loch and elsewhere, he noted that on all too many occasions when people tried to photograph the monsters of the deep, their cameras failed to work properly, or the photographs came out fogged or blurry when they were developed. Holiday admitted that most Loch Ness Monster researchers dismissed such anomalies as anything other than mere chance, primarily because the overriding viewpoint was that physical animals—even ones of an unknown type—simply did not have the ability to cause cameras to malfunction. And yet, the sheer, illogical number of reports on file in which camera-related problems were so prevalent added weight to Holiday's growing beliefs that there was something very, very unsettling about the long-necked creatures that have, for so long, called Loch Ness their home.

The most disturbing aspect of Holiday's research was still to come, however. One day in 1973, not long after the series of exorcisms performed by the Reverend Dr. Donald Omand, Holiday was once again at Loch Ness, still faithfully seeking the truth about his enigmatic, elusive nemeses. He later recorded that on the day in question, "...across the grass, beyond the roadway and at the top of the slope leading down to Loch Ness...stood a figure. It was a man dressed entirely in black. Unlike other walkers who sometimes pause to admire the Loch Ness panorama, this one had his back to the loch and was staring fixedly at me" (Holiday 1986).

Echoing what so many others have said about the Men in Black, Holiday admitted to feeling a deep sense of malevolence and abnormality emanating from the cold, passionless entity in his presence. Suddenly, Holiday heard a curious whispering or whistling noise, and the Man in Black vanished in an instant. Later, there was a near-fatal sequel to this disquieting event: When he returned to Loch Ness in 1974 to continue his investigations, Holiday was stopped in his tracks after only a few days with a serious heart attack. As a stretcher carried him up the edge of the loch to a waiting ambulance, he peered groggily over the side and noted that he had just passed over the exact same spot where the Man in Black had stood the previous year.

Sadly, Holiday passed away prematurely in 1979; he was not even 60. Some might be inclined to suspect that he was a victim of the Men in Black.

May 3, 1975 was the date of a truly memorable UFO encounter, complete with MIB, that was brought to the attention of Dr. Josef Allen Hynek, who acted as a scientific advisor for the U.S. Air Force's UFO investigation programs Sign, Grudge, and Blue Book, and who, in 1973, had founded the Center for UFO Studies. The unfortunate figure that got caught up in this mystery was a man named Carlos Antonio de los Santos Montiel, who had a close encounter of the UFO kind after taking to the skies from Mexico City in his Piper Aztec 24 aircraft. It was while in the vicinity of Tequesquitengo that his aircraft was briefly surrounded by three small saucer-shaped vehicles that shadowed him *extremely* closely. Disturbingly, those same UFOs, as they surrounded Montiel's aircraft, seemingly elevated it from 15,000 feet to 15,800 feet (4,572 m to 4,816 m), before soaring away into the skies towards the Popocatepetl and Iztaccihuatal volcanoes. That experience was nothing compared to what happened next.

Hynek (who passed away in 1986) said that several weeks after his encounter Montiel was supposed to appear on a Mexican television show to talk about his UFO experience. He never showed up at the studio. Montiel claimed that his car had been forced off the road while he was driving to the station. A strange-looking man dressed in black clothing approached Montiel after he successfully brought his car to a halt, and suggested in stern tones that it would be most unwise for him to go on the show. Montiel chose to follow the man's advice—and, just maybe, it saved Montiel's life.

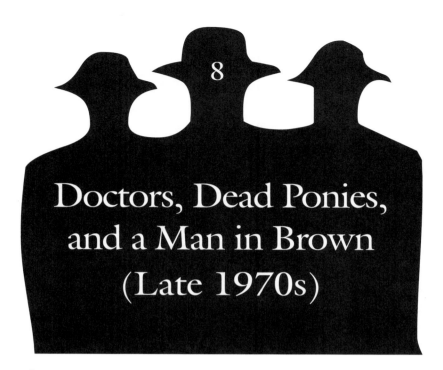

8

Doctors, Dead Ponies, and a Man in Brown (Late 1970s)

A sinister MIB case rivaling that of Albert Bender in high strangeness occurred around 8 p.m. on the evening of September 11, 1976. Hours earlier, Dr. Herbert Hopkins could never have guessed that his world was about to be plunged into chaos, but that is precisely what fate had in store for him. Hopkins, a general practitioner who lived in Orchard Beach, Maine, had experience in the field of hypnosis, and had then recently subjected to regression therapy an alleged alien abductee named David Stephens. It was in October 1975 that Stephens, a resident of the nearby town of Oxford, suffered from a period of missing time after an experience with anomalous aerial lights while driving late at night. In an attempt to open the door to the hidden depths of Stephens's mind, and to try and determine what had really happened to him, Hopkins ultimately opened the door of his own home to a Man in Black.

On the night in question, Hopkins was home alone when the telephone rang. On the other end was some-one claiming to represent the New Jersey UFO Research Organization, who wished to speak with the doctor about the Stephens case. Hopkins did not know it at the time, but there *was* no New Jersey UFO Research Organization. Had he known that, it's highly unlikely that Hopkins would ever have considered doing what he chose to do next: He invited the man over, right then and there. This in itself was very curious and totally illogical, Hopkins later realized, as he did not even think to ask the man's name. Also, the Hopkins home had been broken into on two occasions, which made his actions even more puzzling—and reckless. As a result of Hopkins's invite, the voice at the end of the phone soon arrived on the scene. In fact, he arrived *too* soon.

Because it was already after 8 p.m. and the skies were dark, after hanging up the telephone Hopkins went to the door and turned on the outside light, to provide his visitor with some illumination when he finally arrived. To Hopkins's astonishment, however, the Man in Black was *already there*, making his slow, steady way up the porch stairs and directly toward the stunned doctor. Oddly, there was no parked car in sight, and Hopkins knew there was no telephone booth close by from where the man could have conceivably gotten to his residence with such mystifying speed. Even odder, Hopkins simply opened the door wide and let the man in.

The identity of the man did not become any clearer when he entered the Hopkins residence. Perhaps it was the unsettling appearance of the caller from the darkness that helped ensure that Hopkins totally forgot to secure a name: The man's clothes and Homburg hat were utterly black, his suede gloves were gray, his skin was deathly white, and his body was skinny in the extreme—as was evidenced by the fact that the man's wrinkle-free suit was clearly way too large for his sickly looking, skeletal frame. More astonishing, when the man sat down and removed his Homburg, Hopkins could not fail to see that he was totally devoid of any hair on his head. There was not even any telltale stubble. In addition, he lacked both eyebrows and eyelashes. The man's bright red, extremely thin lips stood out dramatically in contrast to his milk-white skin.

A sure sign that something awful and inhuman had entered the Hopkins abode was the reaction of the family's dog, which was part German shepherd and part collie. It barked furiously as the man came into the living room, then put its tail between its legs and raced off to the safety of a nearby closet, where it shakily remained for the duration of the mystery man's visit. The Man in Black was seemingly unfazed by the actions of the frightened hound; he got directly to the point and began questioning Hopkins about his work on the alien-abduction experience of David Stephens. Even the mode of questioning struck Hopkins as strange: The man had no detectable accent, was entirely unemotional and monotone, and seemed robotic in his physical appearance and mannerisms. Strangest of all, at one point, as he listened carefully to Hopkins, the Man in Black placed the backs of his fingers to his lips. Hopkins noted with amazement that the gray gloves the man was wearing quickly became stained red; this unusual character was wearing bright red lipstick.

Things then seemed to go from plain odd to distinctly sinister. The dark visitor told Hopkins that he, Hopkins, had two coins in the left pocket of his pants, which, amazingly, turned out to be true. The mysterious guest then told rather than asked Hopkins to take one of the coins out of his pocket and hold it in the palm of his hand, which he duly did. Laying on the orders even thicker, the Man in Black then instructed Hopkins not to look in his direction, but to carefully keep his eye fixed on the coin. Hopkins could only watch, awestruck, as the silver coin took on a blue color, became blurry, changed from metallic form to a vaporous substance, and finally faded into nothingness.

This strange character then suddenly made a less-than-veiled threat to Hopkins. He told the doctor that Barney Hill—the husband of famed 1961 alien abductee Betty Hill, about whom we will learn more in a later chapter—had died because he had no heart, just as Hopkins now no longer had the coin. A feeling of pure dread came over the doctor.

The Man in Black then ordered Hopkins to destroy any and all data relative to the David Stephens affair; otherwise Hopkins would surely be bound to follow the same fate that befell Barney Hill. (In reality, Hill's death was *not* due to any heart-related ailment at all; his premature passing, in 1969, was actually the result of a cerebral hemorrhage.) Ensuring that he did as he was told, Hopkins was strongly warned by the Man in Black that he would definitely know if Hopkins had followed his instructions—or had not.

Then came what was perhaps the most bizarre aspect of the evening: The speech of the man suddenly began to noticeably slow down; he stood up on what Hopkins could see were clearly unsteady feet, and made his way to the door, which Hopkins opened for him. Gripping the railing tightly, the Man in Black departed with a clumsily worded claim that his energy was running low. An astonished Hopkins could only watch with a mixture of fear and trepidation as the man took slow, cautious steps toward a very bright light that illuminated the driveway to such an extent that Hopkins could not make out what was responsible for the intense glow—only that it was no car. Or, at least, it was no *normal* car. Hopkins raced to the kitchen window to try to get a better view of the scene, but both the curious caller and the light had vanished in the few seconds it took Hopkins to reach the kitchen.

By the time his wife and children returned home from seeing a movie, Hopkins was in a state of considerable distress and near-panic. After telling them of what had occurred, he wasted no time in demagnetizing all the tapes of the interviews he had conducted with David Stephens, and then, just for good measure, threw the tapes into the roaring fireplace, where they were soon forever destroyed, as were Hopkins's precious notes and files. Such a thorough cleansing, Hopkins earnestly prayed, would bring things to a halt. It did not. For almost a full week afterward, Hopkins had terrifying nightmares during the early hours in which the face of the Man in Black loomed before him and over him, getting ever bigger and ever closer. And the family was briefly cursed with a prevalent calling card of the Men in Black: widespread telephone interference.

It was all quite enough, unsurprisingly, for Dr. Herbert Hopkins to walk away from the David Stephens affair without even a single look back. There is, however, one final point worth noting. It relates to the ability of the Man in Black to transform one of the coins taken from Hopkins's pocket into a vaporous substance. And it is a point that suggests the MIB phenomenon may be much older than we actually suspect. It comes from Men in Black authority Brad Steiger: "Many of the great alchemists—a subject I'm fascinated by—were seeking to find angels that they could command. Magic is seen as an unapproved ritual when it's to bring profit to oneself, but they were seeking to command these entities to bring them forth the secret to turn base metals into precious metals. I have found a number of instances where alchemists were visited by a gentleman in black, a prosperous burgher in black, who appeared in the laboratory and demonstrated certain things to them. Some are benevolent and some are more sinister."

Sinister men dressed in black, of the type Steiger describes—that had the ability to morph metals, and during mysterious visitations subsequently demonstrated such skills—sound astonishingly like centuries-old versions of Dr. Herbert Hopkins's very own manipulator, or in this case destroyer, of metal.

I am also conversant with the facts surrounding the experience of yet another doctor with the MIB in the mid-1970s, also in the United States, in a small town in northern Idaho. In this instance, the doctor (who requested anonymity here) was asked to conduct an examination of a young boy's arm that had been marked with an unusual abrasion.

"I asked him how he got the strange marks, and what created them. He replied, 'The space doctors.'" As the doctor listened, the boy related seeing a "low-flying airplane" enter a secluded area of woodland near his home. Curious as to what was going on, the boy ventured into the woods and came across a group of strange-looking people who, said the doctor, "captured" the boy, transferred him to some form of craft, and subjected him to "countless medical and intelligence tests."

All of this could have been considered nothing more than the result of an overactive imagination on the part of the boy. Five years later, however, an event occurred that cast such a down-to-earth scenario into major doubt. The doctor was at home, watching television, when there was a knock at the door. There, before the doctor, were two men dressed in "black jumpsuits, black shoes, and black gloves and even sunglasses."

Only one spoke, and inquired as to whether or not the doctor had "known of the boy." The doctor asked why the two MIB wanted to know, and the response of the talkative one was that he was merely curious. Naturally suspicious, the doctor related only part of the story as it related to the boy, after which one of the MIB managed a slight emotionless smile. Both then quickly departed, never again to darken the doctor's door.

The morning of April 11, 1977, was a very strange one: No less than 15 wild ponies were found dead at Cherry Brook Valley, Dartmoor, Devonshire, England, by a Tavistock shopkeeper, Alan Hicks, who had been crossing the bleak, windswept, ancient moors with his children. It was not until mid-July, however, that the media began reporting on the incident in depth. Newspaper articles in my possession show that the story traveled as far as South Africa. Indeed, the Durban *Daily News* recorded on July 15, "Men in masks using metal detectors and a Geiger counter yesterday scoured a remote Dartmoor valley in a bid to solve a macabre mystery. Their search centered on marshy grassland where 15 wild ponies were found dead, their bodies mangled and torn" ("UFO link with pony deaths" 1977).

While other investigators were looking for evidence of malnutrition, disease, poisoning, or even gunshot wounds, these four men were seeking proof that visiting extraterrestrials were responsible for the deaths. If a UFO *had* been in the vicinity, suggested John Wyse, the founder of the Devon UFO Center, to which the four men were attached, it was not at all inconceivable that evidence of such a landing just might still be discernible, although none was ever found. According to the Dartmoor Pony Society, however, the ponies had probably died natural deaths on various parts of the moors and had been simultaneously dumped together by a farmer unwilling to bear the cost of their burials.

Numerous other theories were postulated at the time, but the trail went cold until 1991, when Jonathan Downes, a prolific author, journalist, and investigator, began to probe the case. Downes—who was living in Devonshire at the time (and resides there to this day)—succeeded in tracking down a number of those people who had been quoted by the newspapers some 14 years previously. Curiously, Downes detected a distinct reluctance to talk, even after almost a decade and a half. Even more bizarre, one of those same individuals, who strictly adhered to a non-paranormal explanation for the pony deaths, complained to a research colleague of Downes's about constantly pestering her day and night, when in actuality the only contact had been one solitary telephone call.

As Downes noted, this was all reminiscent of the Men in Black–related experiences of the writer John Keel, who stated in his book, *The Mothman Prophecies*, with regard to such annoying and mysterious telephone victimization, "I kept a careful log of the crank calls I received and eventually catalogued the various tactics of the mysterious pranksters. Some of these tactics are so elaborate they could not be the work of a solitary nut harassing UFO believers in his spare time. Rather it all appears to be the work of either paranormal forces, or a large and well-financed operation by a large and well-financed organization with motives that evade me" (Keel 1991).

The 1977 pony deaths were never resolved, and, with the investigation of Jonathan Downes having eventually hit the proverbial brick wall, the telephone assault duly faded away, too.

The Men in Black were still out in force as the 1970s came to an end. A researcher named Richard D. Seifried recalled an incident that occurred in 1979 when two MIB were present at a lecture on UFOs in Ohio. According to Seifried, both were dressed in "very neat, dark suits [and] sported GI haircuts and what looked like Air Force regulation dress shoes" (Seifried 1993).

At the end of the lecture, Seifried and his friends left the hall, and, while walking along a long corridor toward a parking area outside, saw the two men directly in front of them. "They rounded the corner," recalled Seifried. "Although we were probably no more than 40 or 50 feet (12 or 15 m) behind them, by the time we turned the corner the two men had disappeared…what they did was inhuman" (Seifried 1993). This experience, it will be noted, is *very* reminiscent of that of Allen Greenfield who, a decade earlier, in 1969, had a Man in Black encounter at a conference on UFOs in Charleston, West Virginia. And, just as was the case with Seifried, Greenfield's Man in Black eerily vanished into nothingness when he tried to quickly pursue him.

That same year, 1979, was notable for one more encounter with a Man in Black—or, rather, in this particular case, a Man in Brown! The witness was a young newsboy named Warren Weisman, who was delivering newspapers on his regular route in Tuscon, Arizona, early on the morning of February 19. Suddenly, and seemingly out of nowhere, a strange object crashed from the skies into a car parked at the side of the road. Such was the ferocity of the impact that it destroyed the back section of the vehicle; the right rear wheel was wrenched from the chassis, and the mysterious device bounced off the car and slammed into a nearby mailbox, knocking it to the ground.

A shocked Weisman tentatively approached the scene of all the mayhem and could see that the object, whatever its nature, was black in color, shiny, and shaped somewhat like a microwave oven. Weisman stood there for a moment, wondering what to do next; that is, until a dark-colored car appeared out of nowhere and pulled up next to him, and out stepped the Man in Brown, who Weisman later described as being a scrawny FBI-type. The Man in Brown, in a fashion that made it sound far more along the lines of a stern order than a friendly suggestion, advised Weisman to continue with his newspaper deliveries. Instead, Weisman raced to the safety of his home, leaving the Man in Brown far behind. It was a very wise move, one suspects.

Colin Bennett Meets Mr. X (Early 1980s)

C olin Bennett is a true visionary in the field of ufological research, interpretation, and writing, who once had an experience with a Man in Black in Notting Hill, an area of West London, England. "Exact dates and times have gone from me now," Bennett says, "but it was in the early 1980s when I met a Man in Black. It was a Sunday, I remember, which was particularly quiet, with no phone calls and no one calling at the flat. This silence was most strange since Notting Hill is an area which in those days could, in five minutes, turn into a cross between a Mexico City shoot-out and a riot in the Old Bazaar in Cairo." Possibly as a hint of what was soon to occur, Bennett notes, "The lack of such activity on this particular Sunday was somewhat unnerving."

Bennett decided that to escape the lack of anything meaningful to do, or anyone to hang out with, he would pay a visit to his local cinema, the Coronet. Afterward, he headed home, at around 11 p.m. It was then that

95

something truly odd occurred. As he was about to enter his apartment, Bennett saw "a great light in the sky straight ahead. This light had peculiar characteristics. It was so powerful that had it been a searchlight, I would have been seriously eye-damaged. But no; despite its size and apparent intensity, the light had a soft, relaxing ambience. I shouted down to the basement of the house where Mary, my girlfriend at the time, lived. She came out, and, illuminated by the glow, started to walk up the steel stairs to pavement level."

Then something bizarre occurred. The unidentified light changed into something radically different: a Second World War–era British Lancaster bomber aircraft, an aircraft that played an integral role in the conflict with Nazi Germany! Not only that, but the aircraft appeared to be *hovering* in the sky over Powis Square: "I turned to the right, thinking to myself, *If Mary doesn't see what I am seeing, then I will have to get medical help.* But fortunately for me, she *did* see the bomber as she reached pavement level," says Bennett.

Colin Bennett's Man in Black encounter was preceded by his sighting of a phantom Lancaster bomber.

It was clear to Bennett that this was *not* some surviving Lancaster that was being flown to or from an aerospace museum or some similar locale. Indeed, whereas the device *looked* like a decades-old wartime bomber, its actions suggested this was not the case, as Bennett clearly and quickly realized: The aircraft was silent, there was no movement from its propellers, and there was no evidence of any insignia or undercarriage. If that was not strange enough, the light that had first morphed into the form of a Second World War bomber then altered its appearance yet again. This time it took on the form of a distinctly triangular-shaped craft, and accelerated out of the area at high speed, in a northerly direction.

"But there were more wonders to come," says Bennett, in what is certainly an understatement: "Lo, upon entering Mary's flat there was a Man in Black sitting on the settee. Mary nervously introduced me, though to this day neither of us can remember his name—another mystery. She said that the man—let's call him Mr. X—had called to see a man named John who lived directly above in the ground-floor flat, but John happened not to be in. Mr. X had, therefore, asked Mary—through the door speaker-phone—if he might wait in her flat for a short while pending the arrival of John. She had agreed to this, and opened the door to let him in, a feature of the scene which was astonishing to me. Notting Hill, as I have said, was an extremely dangerous place to live in at this time, and no lone woman—young or old—in her right mind would ever let a stranger into her dwelling place late at night under any circumstances."

This clear example of a curious lack of any sense of thought for one's personal, physical safety when dealing with the Men in Black mirrors to a truly uncanny degree the 1976 case of Dr. Herbert Hopkins of Maine. One might be inclined to strongly suspect that these black figures hold some sort of sway over our mental faculties and our ability to think logically and coherently.

Bennett says of the enigmatic visitor: "Our Man in Black was quite friendly and affable. An educated, sophisticated person, he had a good English educated accent. However, his appearance fitted parts of the MIB formula: aged around late 30s to early 40s, bronze-blond hair falling down his shoulder in curls and a tanned face. True to form our Mr. X wore a smartly cut jet-black suit with neat black tie and white shirt."

Bennett and Mary then chose to tell Mr. X all about the fantastic, shape-shifting vehicle they had just seen in the skies over Notting Hill. His response, however, was probably not the one that the pair was anticipating: He did not crack a joke, was not even mildly amused, but was certainly not dismissive of the affair either. In fact, Bennett reveals something very interesting and illuminating: "I am being careful not to push the argument here—I got the impression that he knew *all* about what we had just seen. He received our experience in *far too calm* and collected a manner for my taste. He was almost like a professor who was calmly considering the points of an essay that had just been read to him by a student and was ready to give grades. I got the impression that he was checking out our reactions, and that the suit and tie, hair and face, were disguises."

Bennett adds that he was not frightened by the Man in Black, and in no way did the man suggest, in the formulaic sense, that Bennett and Mary should forget about what they had just seen. Rather, Bennett recalls, "After a brief, witty chat, he said that he had decided not to wait for John, and he would be on his way. It was as if he had heard what he wanted to hear and John had become irrelevant. Politely thanking Mary for letting him stay for a while, he disappeared into the Notting Hill night, which, as usual, just happened to be aglow with the blue lights of police vans, instead of the lights from UFOs."

Paralleling almost precisely the way in which Allen Greenfield's dark character seemingly immediately vanished into nothingness back in 1969, and the way Richard D. Seifried's pair of MIB disappeared 10 years later, so Bennett's Man in Black performed a mystifying maneuver, as he reveals: "As soon as Mary closed the door, I got up, opened the door, and our visitor was gone. In Isaac Newton's universe I should have caught our Man in Black going across the yard and up the basement steps, but no, he wasn't there. I asked a gaggle of policeman if they had seen anyone coming up the basement steps. But they had seen no one, and gave menacing glances at my hippie-length hair of those days. Under these circumstances, asking if they had seen a disappearing Man in Black would not have been wise."

By this time, the fact that the man had vanished from sight under very curious circumstances, and the utter illogicality of Mary having casually invited a stranger—and a black-suited stranger at that—into her home with nary a thought for her own safety, were both starting to play deeply on Bennett's swirling mind:

> I sat Mary down and calmly interrogated her. Why had she let him in? She did not know why. I got a little angry and told her she could have

been murdered. She became very upset at the whole business and I decided to pressure her no longer. I should add that Mary was a well-educated girl with a degree in physics. She was a confident and alert woman, somewhat conservative, and a Notting Hill veteran in the bargain. Her behavior on this occasion was most peculiar. I then realized that she was in shock, and I stopped applying pressure. This was the beginning of a fracture in the relationship which I believe to this day was caused by the UFO/MIB incident.

The most fantastic aspect of the story was still to come, however. It is an aspect that Bennett has never forgotten: "I made my way back to my own flat on the second floor. I bent down to put food into the cat dish. As I straightened up I knew I had lost some time. By my three clocks and wristwatch it was still 11:05 pm—the time I left the cinema! It was impossible to square the time from my purchase of the cat food to the walk back to the flat—20 minutes in all. I phoned Mary and said I wanted to talk about this, but she refused." (There is a particularly novel theory to explain time displacement and manipulation as they relate to the Men in Black, which will become apparent in a later chapter.) The next day, Bennett "met with the said John and told him that I had met a friend of his the previous evening. I described our MIB to him, and John said he did not have any kind of friend who corresponded remotely to that description. Well there we are—a UFO, a Man in Black, and a girlfriend who no longer would have anything to do with me!"

Bennett concedes, nearly **30** years later, "I am well aware that skeptics might say that as regards the Man in Black, I had experienced my own form of hallucination." Countering such an argument, or the notion that the whole thing was some big laugh at his expense, Bennett makes a very good point: "But if he was some joker, how he got past Mary, how he synchronized his arrival with the sky display, and how he made me feel I had lost some time remains a mystery to me."

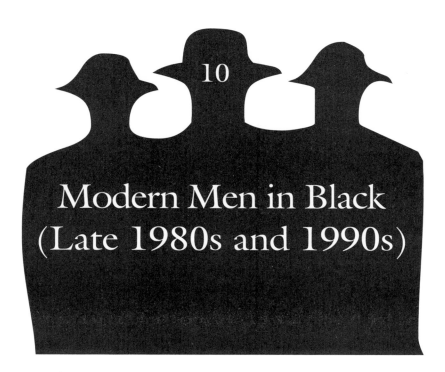

10

Modern Men in Black (Late 1980s and 1990s)

In the late 1980s, and mid- to late 1990s, there occurred a veritable wave of Men in Black activity across both the United States and Great Britain that was directly linked with the so-called alien-abduction phenomenon. There were the typical threats, both in person and via telephone; mail went missing, or at the very least showed clear evidence of tampering; and deep paranoia overwhelmed certain players in the sagas. All the while, the Men in Black looked on with icy, approving eyes at the chaos and mental carnage they were generating.

From respected investigator Peter Hough comes a truly remarkable account with ties to the Men in Black. Of the many and varied cases that Hough investigated, one concerned a police officer, Philip Spencer, who in 1987 allegedly stumbled across an apparent alien creature on Ilkley Moor, Yorkshire, England. Hough's investigation suggested that Spencer had suffered a degree of missing time—of the type that is typical of alien-abduction

103

incidents—but the most notable aspect of the story was an amazing piece of evidence that Spencer had at his disposal to back up his extraordinary claim: a solitary photograph displaying a small, dark-colored creature striding up a grassy slope on the moors.

In an attempt to determine what had occurred during the period of missing time, Spencer was hypnotically regressed, and recalled being taken onboard a large, silver-colored flying saucer, where he underwent some form of physical examination, and was given a warning about a future ecological disaster that would affect the Earth. More significantly, the regression allowed Spencer to accurately recall in his mind the image of the alien entity that he encountered: It was small in height, somewhere in the region of 4 feet (1.2 m); it had pointed ears, large eyes, a small mouth, huge hands, and three fingers on each hand that reminded Spencer of large sausages.

But that was not all. Guess who was soon to put in an appearance? Yes, you guessed right. On a Friday evening in January 1988, events took an even stranger turn for Spencer. Hearing a knock at his front door, Spencer duly opened it, only to find himself confronted by two middle-aged men, dressed smartly in business suits. Ominously, both flashed Ministry of Defense identity cards bearing the names Jefferson and Davis.

Spencer, puzzled and even somewhat alarmed, duly invited the men in and carefully listened as Jefferson announced that they had come to interview him about his UFO experience on the moors the previous year. Even more odd, Spencer had only discussed his encounter with three civilian UFO investigators; yet the men from the Ministry—or *allegedly* from the Ministry—apparently knew all about his experience and fired off a barrage of pointed questions and demands to the perplexed officer in relation to his UFO encounter.

Perhaps mindful of the fact that he was dealing with officialdom, Spencer admitted to having taken one photograph, but stated that it was in the possession of a friend. In reality, however, the negative was in Peter Hough's hands at the time in question. With this revelation, the two men suddenly lost all interest in further communication and quickly left as mysteriously as they had first arrived. Was this, perhaps, because they realized they were too late to retrieve Spencer's potentially priceless evidence of his alien abduction? Who were the mysterious pair? Were they, possibly, covert operatives of the British government? Or did they have origins of a much stranger nature? To this day, the true identities of Jefferson and Davis remain mysterious.

Moving on almost a decade, we have yet another case from the British Isles. Irene Bott, formerly the president of the Staffordshire UFO Group, investigated a notable case implicating the Men in Black in the alien-abduction controversy. Shortly after establishing her group in 1995, Bott was plunged into a situation involving a witness to a UFO who may very well have also undergone a period of so-called missing time. Expressing deep desire to learn more about what occurred to him than the fragmentary memories that were circulating around his brain, the witness contacted Bott and related the details that surrounded his viewing, in the early hours of a 1995 morning, of a brightly lit, triangular-shaped object in the low skies of the county of Staffordshire.

The witness was certain that there was more to the case than he could consciously recollect, and expressed a keen desire for help in unraveling what had really taken place. As a result, Bott referred the witness to a colleague in her group, and the two discussed the details over the telephone. Crucial to the issues under discussion in this book is this: Shortly after returning home from work one day, the witness found that a note had been pushed through his mailbox warning him not to proceed any further with the investigation of his UFO encounter.

Naturally deeply concerned, the man asked his neighbors if they had seen anyone lurking in the vicinity of his house who might conceivably have been responsible for the strange and unsettling note. Fortunately, one neighbor *had* seen something unusual that day. Shortly after the witness had set off for work, a black car pulled up outside his house. A man dressed entirely in black and carrying an equally black briefcase exited the vehicle, marched quickly up the driveway, shoved a piece of paper through the full mailbox, hastily returned to the car, and drove off at speed. That's right: One of our mysterious characters had struck again. And it was an encounter that justifiably led Irene Bott to ask the still-unresolved question: "Was this a British Man in Black?"

Moving across the Atlantic and back to the United States, a classic MIB case comes from Marie Jones, a prolific author on countless things both paranormal and mysterious, who says, "I've always had a big interest in unusual phenomena, and alternative things. But, with UFOs, I got involved with the Center for UFO Studies in the late 1970s, and I was also in MUFON—the Mutual

UFO Network—for a good 15 years. But it was in the mid-1990s, after I returned to San Diego after living in Los Angeles that I had some very weird experiences that sound like something to do with the Men in Black."

Author Marie Jones had a run-in with the MIB while investigating alien abductions in the 1990s.

It all began, says Jones, in 1995, when she placed an advertisement in a free local newspaper asking for people to get in touch if they were interested in UFOs. It was an action that proved costly with respect to Jones's emotional state of mind. "From that ad," Jones reveals, "a woman contacted me, whom I'd prefer not to name, but whom I'll call Anna. She was like a biker chick. We really hit it off and we decided to form a group and it took off really quickly; we were very active and did a lot of investigations, particularly with alien-abduction cases and witnesses."

As the two got to know one another, Anna confided in Jones that she was experiencing some serious harassment that sounded very much like classic MIB tactics.

Strange people were telephoning their house, and there were knocks at the door from curious-looking characters. Jones adds with regard to this aspect of the story, "She and her husband lived in a semi-rural area, so they were a bit isolated, which made it more worrying. There were threats on the phone, strange issues with the phone like unusual noises on the line and electronic interference, and things like that. And the more we talked and I got to know her, the more these things started to happen to my phone."

Jones, at least partly as a result of her friendship with Anna, it seems, was now herself a target of the Men in Black. Nevertheless, being of a strong and determined character, Jones was not about to let a bunch of skinny, pasty, black-suited souls from who-knows-where push her around. That's not to say the calls weren't disconcerting, however. "It was always a male caller," she said, "and the person on the other end had a very robotic voice. They almost sounded like they were talking through some kind of voice changer. It was very stilted, very robotic. This person was telling me what clothes I had on, what book I was reading, what room I was in. And the place where I lived, you couldn't see in to it. The calls kept coming and this person was telling me more and more personal things that he never should have known."

Carefully and deliberately instilling in Jones's mind the notion that her every move was being scrutinized by all-powerful, unseen eyes of a potentially deadly nature can only be interpreted as a classic scare tactic—at which, as we have seen, the Men in Black are adept. Jones, tired and fried by the whole situation, wanted hard answers as to what was afoot and why she and Anna were being targeted: "So I started asking Anna if she knew anything about these calls. She said that yes, she had been getting similar calls with a really robotic voice. But she also said that some of the people she had seen—she'd seen them on her property late at night, and her husband would run outside with a gun—moved like robots. They were very stiff, very stilted, and stared without blinking their eyes. But they looked human."

As the high strangeness continued, Jones became even more concerned and affected by the way in which her previously orderly world was rapidly plunging into unrelenting chaos, disorder, and stark terror: "I told my husband at the time, 'Don't answer the phone!' But, looking back, it was crazy that I was even thinking like that. I mean, you *have* to answer the phone, but it really intimidated me. And some of the calls were late at night when my husband—who was a musician—would be gone rehearsing or playing. And this person would always know when I was alone. *Always*. It was *very* strange; I could *not* get rid of this feeling that there was something not right. It wasn't just the way his voice sounded; it was the whole atmosphere. It was horrible."

Jones has her own thoughts on the nature of the mysterious man's agenda. Unsurprisingly, she concludes that the tone, nature, and modus operandi of the Man in Black seemed to radiate both hostility and threat. And many of those threats seemed to be directly linked to Jones's studies of alien-abduction cases and data:

> I believe that what he was trying to do was to let me know that he knew a lot about me and could hurt me if he wanted to. He never actually outright said anything like he would hurt

me, but that was *definitely* the idea he was getting across. It was an insinuation. It was creepy. Looking back on it, the interesting thing is that he was less interested in talking about UFOs as a subject, but much more interested in talking about the group and what the group was doing with our abduction research.

And this man, instead of asking about UFOs, would say something like, "Your group is familiar with this abductee or that abductee," or with this person or that person. He was letting me know that he knew what the group was doing. I have no idea where he was getting the information from, unless he had my phone tapped. And he was even telling me things about what I'd done back in my 20s, what book I had lying on the bed, and what I was wearing at the time. It just gave me the creeps; *very* creepy.

Eventually the situation began to take its toll on both Anna and Jones, to the point that there really seemed to be only one viable option left available to the pair: Somewhat reluctantly, they elected to close down their research group, and Jones moved back to Los Angeles to live. She says today of Anna and the whole experience with the Men in Black: "I have no idea of what became of her, but I can tell you that I am not someone who is easy to intimidate. I'm very confrontational; I'll fight. But this person scared me so much that I literally walked away from my group. And I've never had that happen before. It was a weird kind of foreboding feeling. It made me want to back away and get this person out of my life. I even felt that something not right was going to happen; it was awful."

Investigative author Chris O'Brien has a similar account to relate that also focuses on the MIB/alien-abduction connection. In this particular case, the female witness was referred to him by an unusual source: a sheriff's office in Colorado, O'Brien's state of residency. He takes up the story: "One of the things she mentioned happened right when we were having all sorts of intense waves of UFO activity, in the spring of '94 and through the fall of '95, in the San Luis Valley of Colorado. She kept a very extensive journal, and I cross-referenced some of her claims with our reports and, sure enough, there was a definite correlation. When she would claim to have these UFO experiences, these abductions, we would get UFO sightings reported to us on the exact same nights, but from *other* people—which I thought was *very* intriguing and gave some credence to her story, in my mind."

And then there came a deeply worrying development: The woman's mail failed to arrive on a disturbingly regular basis, and she ended up having to file claims with the post office. Then, on one particular day the woman noticed a large black car that looked like it had just been driven out of a 1960s showroom parked at the end of her driveway. Something sinister was going on, she felt. And, given that this involved the Men in Black, could it really have been anything *but* sinister?

O'Brien says of this development, "It looked like a brand-new, old car—which is kind of an oxymoron, but that's what she said. And there were these two guys outside the car whom she said looked like the Blues Brothers, going through her mail—getting it out of the mailbox, opening it, and so on. She was watching all this through a spotting scope and was able to catch some details, but as soon as she started heading down there—she got on her ATV—they took off. This happened a number of times before she had to get a Post Office box in town. But she *still* had problems—not as bad, though—and this went on for about a year before it finally finished."

Fortunately, the woman had been able to get a very good look at the strange pair on one occasion when they raided her mailbox. Based on O'Brien's words, they might very well have stepped straight out of the shadowy confines of poor old Albert Bender's attic: "They had the fedoras, the wrap-around shades, the skinny ties; it was the whole Men in Black deal. I tried to get her to come up with another description, something a bit more credible-sounding than 'like the Blues Brothers.' But, that's all she would say: They looked like Jake and Elwood!"

The experiences of Marie Jones and Chris O'Brien's source may have come to an end, but there are others that still merit our attention. Oregon-based anomalies researcher and writer Regan Lee says of an alien-abductee with whom she had contact in the 1990s, "I'll call her Jane. She had a UFO encounter in the early 1990s in the Gold Hill area campground in Oregon. She recalled through hypnosis and flashbacks that she had been abducted by aliens and given a medical examination. She had several more encounters and UFO sightings, some witnessed by others who were with her."

And, yet again, our old friends were just itching to come looming out of the darkness. "It was while she was experiencing these sightings, encounters, and telepathic communications with entities," Lee says, "she had a strange thing happen with Men in Black, which occurred in the month of July, at the institution at which she was then working."

It was a blistering hot day when Jane's attention was drawn to three tall, golden-skinned, bearded men. They were dressed in black suits, black hats, black shoes, and very heavy, woolen, full-length coats that—surely at this stage of the game I scarcely need to say—were also black in color. Jane pondered the undeniable strangeness of three men in black wool coats in July, and mused upon the possibility that they might be nothing stranger than visiting rabbis, although they seemed far more Asian than Jewish. Jane told Lee that even though the three men were deep in conversation with one another, she was unnerved to see that their eyes were focused intently upon her, and even appeared to be assessing her in some fashion.

Lee elaborates on the nature of the entities that Jane encountered: "They seemed eerily aware of, and interested in Jane. There was no warning or other interaction, or references to UFOs, yet their very presence could be construed as a warning. It served to startle Jane; she associated the encounter with her abductions and sightings. The bearded men suggest, to me, a religious aspect. Jane was a religious person. I don't know for sure, but I think she was a Mormon. Were the beards connected with that somehow? Maybe they used Jane's religious frame of reference to get her attention."

A few weeks later, says Lee, Jane was listening to a radio talk-show in her car, when one particular caller related over the airwaves her very own UFO experience in Colorado. The caller's encounter was followed by a visit from three men dressed completely in black clothing. Not surprisingly, Lee reveals, "This story gave Jane a jolt, wondering if the three Men in Black she saw weren't the same phenomena. Jane wondered if she hadn't been 'marked or implanted' by the aliens and if she was being followed."

In other words, a typical side effect of the MIB experience—paranoia—had infected yet another unfortunate soul.

Then there is the 1996 experience of Greg Bishop, a prolific author and researcher on a wide range of topics, including UFOs, psychedelics, and conspiracy theories. Bishop's account is a fascinating one, as it also contains an integral ingredient of Chris O'Brien's revelations—namely, the involvement of MIB-style characters rummaging through the mail of individuals intimately linked to the alien-abduction controversy. Significantly, Bishop's story is steeped in distressing paranoia.

Bishop begins thus with his unsettling tale: "Mail tampering is the darling of the clinical paranoids, but nearly every piece of mail that the late researcher and alien-abductee Karla Turner sent to my P.O. box looked like it had been tampered with or opened. Since this is easy to do without having to be obvious, we figured someone was interested in her work enough to make it clear that she was being monitored. She took to putting a piece of transparent tape over the flap and writing 'sealed by sender' on it. Karla pretty much took it for granted after awhile, and suggested I do likewise."

It was unnerving experiences such as those with Karla Turner that had a profoundly negative psychological effect on Bishop and his state of mind at the time. In a frank and open fashion, Bishop states today, "During my extremely horrible paranoid period, when I had a year or two of *ridiculous* paranoia, which would have been about 1996 or '97, I thought there were people taking pictures of the house—which there really were. I actually *did* see somebody once take a picture and quickly drive away. Today, I wonder if it could very well have been real-estate people, but back then, I was like: It's the Men in Black."

And as Bishop saw more and more demons hiding under every rock—or, perhaps, more and more Men in Black lurking within the heart of every black shadow and dark recess—things began to get progressively worse. Bishop was on a terrifying downward spiral that showed no signs of ending:

> I thought people were reading my computer screen from outside the house. I thought my landlord upstairs was following me through the house. It was really weird: one night I was up at 2 in the morning and I walked into the bedroom, and I could hear somebody walk into the bedroom upstairs. It was the same apartment floor plan upstairs as mine. For about five minutes, the person walked everywhere I did, right after me. I could hear the floor creaking right above me in every room I went into. Things like this, I built into this framework of paranoia. I was stressed, paranoid, and thinking there were these MIB-types outside the house. Maybe there were. But, you know, whether I was being

watched or not, if you've got a vast, paranoid conspiracy made up in your mind—as I did at the time—then everything fits into it; and it *did* fit with the thing with Karla [Turner] and the mail getting opened.

Thankfully, Bishop was eventually able to take significant steps back from the darkness that was beckoning with bony fingers. The negativity and the cold fear in which he had been enveloped for so long began to ease, and eventually faded away. Today, Bishop—who still plays a significant role in ufological research and writing, but for whom paranoia no longer has any place in his life—says of his year or two of personal turmoil, "I got out of that state of mind for one simple reason: I was just so tired of being paranoid. It wears on you; it makes you physically and mentally tired. It doesn't mean I wasn't being watched, or that there weren't mail problems. *There were*. But, I couldn't live like that, in fear, any longer."

Unfortunately, as we have seen, not everyone has proven to be quite as lucky as Greg Bishop: The dark and winding highway incessantly traveled by the Men in Black is one littered with disaster, misfortune, and mental collapse.

MIB in the New Millennium (2000s)

Raven Meindel, a cryptozoologist, writer, radio host, and Wiccan priestess who resides in Michigan and, in 2010, was featured on the History Channel's *Monster Quest* series pursuing bloodthirsty werewolves, says, "I've been interested in paranormal things and UFOs for years, but when I got involved in doing it more seriously, with research and writing, and in a career-like manner, that's when *really* strange things started to happen, including a Men in Black experience in April 2008."

Meindel's experience was preceded by a decidedly unusual occurrence in the family home: A week before she had her Men in Black confrontation, her husband, Adam, felt a rush of wind go past him *inside* the apartment, while the pair was standing there, talking. Meindel is sure that the air-conditioning was not on, and no windows were open. It felt, said Adam, just like someone had brushed by, walking briskly past him. Whatever the cause of the

Researcher Raven Meindel, who found herself plagued by the MIB.

odd event, it was an uncanny precursor to the mayhem that was soon to follow, as Meindel makes graphically clear: "On April 16, about 5:30 p.m., two men, dressed all in black, came out of the apartment across from where we were living at the time. The odd thing about this is that no one was living in that apartment then. They walked away and got into a black Lincoln. And when they walked past, I was outside playing with a Frisbee with a neighborhood kid. The Frisbee was called an Alien Flyer, which had an alien face on it, which I thought was a *very* odd synchronicity."

Feeling somewhat unsettled by the off-putting presence of the pair, Meindel tried her best to lighten the situation. Her efforts were to no avail, however. Indeed, no one, I am sure, needs to be told that the Men in Black are hardly known for their fine sense of humor or jollity: "We smiled at the guys, and made a joke about something, but they were like totally stone-cold, chiseled, hard features, no emotion, nothing. One of them looked like he was in his late 20s or early 30s, and the other one was probably late 40s, early 50s. They were all in black and they were both carrying briefcases."

At first, says Meindel, she wondered if the two men were perhaps representatives of some religious group. As there was nothing to indicate that, however, Meindel attempted to move closer to see the license plate of the pair's car as they got inside their black vehicle. Meindel developed a deep suspicion that the pair knew exactly what she was doing, and "they backed out real quick and took off. You could tell it was a deliberate maneuver."

It was in the immediate wake of this chilling MIB experience that a reign of paranormal terror descended upon the Meindel family: The telephone would ring, but—surprise, surprise—no one was there. On the night of April 19, only three days after her encounter with the MIB, and while trying valiantly to fall asleep (which was hardly easy, given the nature of the odd activity in the family home), Meindel developed an overwhelming feeling that she should not be undertaking *any* type of UFO research whatsoever. In her own words, "It was like a terrifying feeling that came on from nowhere. I even felt kind of shaken by it. And I actually said, out loud: 'Okay, I won't do it.'"

Despite her reluctance to dig further into the complexities of the UFO jigsaw, the Men in Black were far from finished toying with, and terrifying, Meindel and her family. Two days later, while Meindel was out walking her dog, something even stranger and scarier happened: a black, luxury-type car, maybe a Cadillac, appeared on the scene and seemed to be shadowing her. She says of this new development: "There was an older man driving and a younger man in the passenger seat. I got a strange sensation. I felt something *very* strange. They pulled up right next to me. It was like the older man was deliberately stopping to let me know they were stopping *for* me, *because* of me—maybe only a foot (2.3 m) from me, right at the edge of the sidewalk."

Meindel's fear levels rose dramatically when one of the men took off his seat belt and appeared ready to get out of the car. At that point, Meindel had an idea: She pulled out her cell phone, so that the pair would clearly understand she was calling someone, and began to walk away from them and toward a nearby clubhouse. "I looked over my shoulder, and finally they did leave, but they were very deliberate in their movements. There's no doubt in my mind they were trying to scare me."

The scare tactics *were* working, and they showed no signs of stopping either. A couple of weeks later, Meindel recalls, her husband, Adam, distinctly heard, on several occasions, whispered voices throughout the apartment. Most disturbing of all was the occasion when, to their horror, the family found what appeared to be very strange handprints on the bathroom mirror: "One was huge, where the fingers had kind of drawn down the mirror," Meindel says. She adds something even more sinister: "My daughter, when she came out of the shower that day, had bruises on her arm that looked *exactly* like the fingerprints on the mirror."

Meindel explained to me that she faithfully recorded all of this undeniably disturbing anomalous activity—that plagued the family for *months*—in the pages of a journal that she had the keen foresight and presence of mind to purchase. Shortly after 2 a.m. on February 11, 2009, Meindel penned the following passage that clearly illustrates the level of high strangeness that had descended upon them:

> *Night Terror*—I'm still very shaken from something that just happened. I'm terribly upset and can't get back to sleep. 1:21 was the last time I looked at the clock before having fallen asleep. The next thing I know I was awake again, and was staring at my bedroom curtain. All of a sudden, this harsh tingling feeling started in my legs and worked its way up my torso and into my head until my whole body was being crushed; lots of pressure and a loud noise was humming in my ear. I was trying hard to scream: 'Adam!' But, I couldn't. I remember looking back toward the curtain and saying to whoever, or whatever, was there: "I hate you!" Then I came out of it, or woke up. I lay there wondering if I had the start of a stroke or an aneurism. I looked at the clock again and it read 1:42 a.m. I'm still woozy and foggy and cannot completely focus my eyes. They feel dry and irritated. I'm really scared and I know I won't sleep anymore tonight.

Did something foul and unspeakable come calling in the early hours of that terrifying morning? And was it linked with the sinister presence of the two Men in Black? Looking back on what occurred, Meindel believes that is *precisely* the nature of what occurred: "I have the feeling that when you investigate these things—UFOs—they become aware of it, and of you. And why I think that is because when we moved to our new house, where we live now, I thought it would be all over. I thought it would leave us alone, because we weren't at the old apartment where it had all happened. But on day two of being here, Adam and I saw this strange red ball of light come right down over us—in the sky, I mean—while we were outside. It felt like someone, or something, was saying, *I'm watching you.*"

Today, Meindel reflects with trepidation upon the horrifying series of experiences that began with the Men in Black and that took a hold of her life for a significant period: "Since this all happened, I have stayed away from the UFO thing. I *do* still dabble in it a bit, but I'm not really researching it deeply anymore. It scared me from going into it any deeper. I got the message, and I'm not going to mess with the UFO thing anymore."

Meindel concludes, in a fashion to which surely the many unfortunate witnesses of the Men in Black can relate, "The fear is still with me."

Situated only a short distance from the city of Albany, New York, the Albany Rural Cemetery was designated in 1841 in response to an ever-growing problem of widespread flooding at cemeteries within the city itself. On October 7, 1844, a dedication marked the opening of this new locale, a tree-filled and tranquil place that houses the remains of a number of historical figures, including Chester A. Arthur, the 21st president of the United States; a noted sculptor named Erastus Dow Palmer; and Daniel Manning, who served under President Grover Cleveland in the position of Secretary of the Treasury.

Also buried within the Albany Rural Cemetery is a Charles Hoy Fort, after whom the renowned monthly magazine on just about everything supernatural, *Fortean Times*, is proudly named. Fort, a dedicated early-20th-century collector and chronicler of stories relative to UFOs, strange creatures, ghosts, paranormal phenomena, and much more, penned a number of highly revered books that carefully recorded his dedicated research, including *Lo!* and *Wild Talents*. It is therefore fitting for a place holding all that is left of this renowned paranormal visionary to also be home to a wide range of supernatural phenomena, including a ghostly black dog, phantom cars, and what is believed to be the spectral remains of a pair of tragic lovers who passed on decades ago, whose souls are forever doomed to wander among the old gravestones.

Against this notable history of connections to all things unsettling, in 2009 the Men in Black decided to put in their own appearance at the cemetery.

"It was May of 2009," says Claudia Cunningham, "and a friend of mine named Linda, who is a registered nurse at the Veteran's Memorial Hospital in Albany, had an encounter with the Men in Black at the cemetery. Last spring she called me and said, 'I know you're interested in this stuff, and you know I'm into the Ouija boards, and I like to go to the card readers, but something *really* weird has happened.' And she wanted to know if I could help her out with it."

That "something *really* weird" to which Linda was referring was nothing less than a dramatic daytime encounter with the Men in Black. Cunningham sets the scene for what was soon to follow:

Albany Rural Cemetery is a very imposing place. It's located on a two-mile (3.2 km) hill, and is full of extremely beautiful crypts holding the aristocracy of the early settlers. With this in mind, Linda decided to go on a little historical tour of her own; this was around 2 p.m. She pulled in the main gate, and you go over a railroad track. And then about 50 feet (15 m), you come to these big wrought-iron gates, which are open during the day. On the left is a very Gothic-looking, round building that contains the records of everyone that's buried there. Across the street from that is the crematorium. The road goes right into the cemetery, and it's a very wide, black macadam road.

When she arrived, Linda spotted from her car what she presumed was a calm and tranquil spot to sit and relax. Unfortunately, it turned out to be the exact opposite. When she looked up again after glancing down to take the keys out of the ignition, her breath was taken away when she saw that, within barely a second or two, a black, military-looking SUV had parked directly behind her. So close was the SUV that Linda told Cunningham it looked like it was practically in the backseat of her car. Quite naturally, Linda's first thought was, *I'm going to get robbed or worse*. So, she put her car in drive, and very slowly crept away from the SUV. "But," explains Cunningham, the SUV "went back up the hill and didn't follow her at all. She watched in her rearview mirror and it looked like the SUV was going down one of the side roads."

Linda, explained Cunningham, is an Italian girl with a temper, and certainly no one was going to put one over on her. So she decided to do a bit of detective work and began to follow the driver of the SUV. When Linda reached a chain-link fence where the road ended, however, the SUV was nowhere in sight; it was almost as if it had vanished, literally. But when Linda headed back to the entry point to the cemetery, she was in for a big surprise: There was the SUV again,

Claudia Cunningham believes the MIB have demonic origins.

parked right in the middle of the road. As if that was not strange enough, Linda then encountered the driver of the mysterious vehicle.

Cunningham recalls what her friend told her: "There was a man, all in black, about 40 years old, black hair—the whole regalia—standing on the side by the driver, and it looked like he was talking to the driver. Linda said to me, 'Very slowly, I pulled up, and he kind of nodded.' And then she jammed the accelerator, and she quickly looked in the mirror, but he was gone—immediately. He was there one second and then gone the next. There was no time for him to run or go anywhere."

"That was enough to really get me going," says Cunningham. "I'm the type that when I get my teeth into something I can't let go until I find out the answer.

So, for a couple of months after that, I would bring it up in conversation with my mother, my boyfriend—people who are open-minded to this stuff. One day—I had moved back in with my mother, who is 95, and I take her shopping every day—I said to her, 'Let's go over to the Delaware Shopping Plaza,' which is about three miles from our house."

It was here that Cunningham went from being someone who had merely been fortunate enough to hear of an encounter with the Men in Black to actually being a direct participant in such an event. "I parked in front of one of the stores," she said. "It was a nice day; I had my windows down and my dog in the car. And to my right there was this big black SUV. I joked to my mother: 'Hey, maybe that's one of those guys that Linda saw.'"

Based upon what happened next, perhaps Cunningham should not have been quick to make light of the situation: "I went into the store, got my purchase, and got back in the car. I was about to turn the key in the ignition and go home. But, from right around the back of the SUV, this little man peeked in the car at me on the passenger's side. He had the black hat—like John Lennon wore in the '60s, the black leather cap that started a whole fashion trend—and he had a three-quarter length black shirt that looked like it just came out of the store, black pants, and black sunglasses. This man steps up on the curb—towards the store—and he just took his glasses down barely an inch and kind of looked right at me and smiled." The smile, recalls Cunningham, "was so creepy." She qualifies this description of the man's facial expression by explaining, "It wasn't scary, but it was like he was saying to me, 'You wanted to see one of these guys—a Man in Black—and so here I am.' So, my take on this is that I believe that you draw to you whatever you believe in. I always wanted some affirmation of Linda's experience, and this was like a confirmation."

For Claudia Cunningham, the experience was undeniable evidence that there is far more to our existence than meets the eye: "I *know* there is a supernatural world. And with the Men in Black, I think they are demonic. They're from the dark side, and here to confuse us. I believe they're here to do a lot of mischief and can take on different forms. They can appear as a ghost, as a Man in Black, an alien. They're here to turn us away from God, and drag us into darker areas."

She continues on this path: "I think the whole UFO phenomenon is demonic and is deceiving us to believe they are aliens. It's all smoke and mirrors. The deception makes it look like they're from another planet and here to silence us about UFOs and aliens. No. This is spiritual. When the Men in Black warn people about UFOs and aliens and why we should not say anything about sightings, our mind is not on the spiritual. They want us to think they are alien; it helps their deception to spread evil and drag people into the occult world." Cunningham's parting words to me were: "Linda got the feeling they were here to do something really awful too. The word she used was *malevolent*. And that's what I think too: malevolent."

> *Before we move on to pastures new—but still, of course, utterly dark in nature—it's worth noting that cases involving Men in Black and their impossibly appearing and disappearing vehicles are quite*

prevalent. For example, Dr. Josef Allen Hynek was provided with the details of a strange MIB encounter that occurred in a small Minnesota town in late 1975 that falls firmly into this category. No UFO was seen on this particular occasion, but a motorist was harassed on a lonely stretch of highway by the driver of a large black Cadillac, which nearly forced the man into an adjacent ditch. The irate man quickly righted his vehicle and headed off in hot pursuit, only to see the black Cadillac lift into the air and, quite literally, disappear in the blink of an eye!

Jenny Randles has investigated a similar case that occurred in Britain in August 1981. In this particular incident, the witness, one Jim Wilson, had seen an unidentified—but not overly fantastic—light in the sky, and was later blessed with a visit from a pair of suit-wearing characters flashing ID cards that demonstrated they came from the British Ministry of Defense. The two suggested to the man that he had merely viewed a Russian satellite—Cosmos 408—and that he should forget all about the experience.

That would indeed have been the end of things, were it not for the fact that Wilson found that, on a number of occasions shortly after the visit occurred, his home seemed to be under some form of surveillance by two men sitting in a black Jaguar (which is the preferred mode of transport in most British Men in Black cases). The police were called, and, across the course of several nights, stealthy checks of the immediate vicinity were made. After seeing the car parked outside Wilson's home on several occasions, and then managing to get a good look at his license plate—which they were quickly able to confirm as being totally bogus—the police carefully closed in, with the intention of speaking with the pair of MIB and finding out the nature of their game. Unfortunately, they never got the chance to do so: As two uniformed officers approached the vehicle and prepared to knock on one of the windows, the black Jaguar melted away into nothingness. There was a deep reluctance on the part of the officers to prepare any written report alluding to such an event!

Just like the Men in Black themselves, even their vehicles are seemingly able to perform ghostly disappearing acts.

Women in Black
(2000)

T hus far, all of the cases we have placed under the microscope have involved *Men* in Black. But what of *Women* in Black? Have such encounters occurred? Yes, they have, although their numbers are certainly less—perhaps barely a handful. Or it might be more accurate to say that *reported* cases involving WIB are far fewer than those involving their male counterparts. Whatever the reason, the infrequency of reports does not detract from their significance. Indeed, as I have noted already in these pages, Albert Bender had a cousin who had received a bedroom visitation from a Woman in Black—although the details are admittedly scant. Far *less* scant in details, however, is the bizarre case of a man named Colin Perks, with whom I met in 2001, before his death in 2009. He had an overriding obsession with finding the final resting place of the legendary King Arthur, which he came to believe was somewhere in the vicinity of an old abbey in the ancient English town of Glastonbury.

The ancient abbey at Glastonbury, England.

In the latter part of 2000, when his investigations into the tales of King Arthur were at their most intense, Perks received an odd, carefully worded telephone call from a woman who said she wished to meet with him to speak about his Arthurian studies. Perks found this highly unsettling, as he had no real family to speak of, and very few of his work colleagues and friends had any significant knowledge of his passion for the tales and mythology surrounding the ancient king. That Perks's enigmatic caller apparently *did* know, however, convinced him to agree to meet with her—at his own home, no less, not far from the legend-filled town of Glastonbury.

At 7 p.m. on the arranged night, there was a loud knock at the front door. Upon opening it, Perks found himself face to face with what he described as the most beautiful woman he had ever seen in his life. Around 6 feet (1.8 m) in height, perhaps 40 years of age, with a head of cascading black hair and milk-colored skin, she wore a chic, expensive-looking black suit. She identified herself as Miss Sarah Key, but, for all intents and purposes she was a Woman in Black. She stood in brief silence, awaiting permission to enter. Precisely as Dr. Herbert Hopkins had done with his Man in Black back in 1976, Perks threw caution to the wind, chose to invite the mysterious visitor into his home, and motioned her into the living room. As the two sat down, the conversation, according to Perks's memory, began something like this: "Mr. Perks, I and several of my colleagues have followed your research closely these last few years."

"That's rubbish," Perks replied. "I've published nothing and spoken to virtually no one. If you know anything about me, you'll know that I keep myself to myself and that's how I like it." Nevertheless, Key replied with a cruel smile, "I *do* know all about you."

As evidence of her claim, the Woman in Black rattled off detail after detail about Perks's quest to find the remains of King Arthur. Key said she was there to express the concerns of a select group of people within the British ruling elite who had a particular interest in certain facets of Perks's dedicated studies.

The story outlined to Perks was mind-blowing. The resting place of King Arthur, he was carefully informed, was also the gateway to a harsh realm populated by nightmarish creatures that would likely provoke catastrophe if allowed entry into our world. Further, prying open Arthur's tomb would ensure the opening of that dreaded door. Thus it was vital that he cease his investigations, she said, lest disaster be unleashed upon the British Isles— and maybe upon the entire planet as well.

According to Perks, at that point, Key drew close to him and said something along the lines of, "Mr. Perks, you cannot begin to understand the enormity of what stands before you. That is why *I* am visiting you and not...

someone else. If you continue and don't let this matter drop, that someone *will* come calling—believe me. And *that* you will *not* want."

Key then stood up and headed for the door. Her demeanor became far more pleasant, and, as Perks recalled it, she said words to the effect of: "That's about it, Mr. Perks. You've done well, but don't go snooping anymore. What you are on the verge of uncovering is the gateway to another world. And you do not want to know what is there, believe me. And we do not want you to open that gateway. Go out and enjoy yourself and put all of this behind you. If you persist, though, you *will* receive another visitor and things will then be out of our control."

Miss Key, a definitively British Woman in Black—who sounds rather like Diana Rigg's character Emma Peel in the classic 1960s TV adventure series *The Avengers*—turned on her black spiked heels, exited the door while Perks stood in silence, and melted into the darkness as enigmatically as she had originally appeared. Unfortunately for Perks, he could not let his research come to a halt after so many years of tirelessly pursuing and trying to unravel the old legends of the fabled king. Having taken the unwise path of ignoring the message of his Woman in Black, Perks *did* receive another visitor—one far different from the alluring Sarah Key.

Around 9 p.m. on a Saturday night in early November 2000, Perks was driving home from the city of Bath along a particularly long stretch of tree-shrouded road. Oddly, given that this was a weekend evening on the fringes of a bustling city, Perks said that he saw absolutely no other cars on the road. He *did* see *something*, however: Suddenly, Perks was confronted by what looked like a large man standing in the middle of the road, straddling the center white line. As Perks slowed his vehicle to a snail's pace, to his terror, he could see that the "man" was actually nothing of the sort.

Pale of skin, it had scrawny arms and legs, and affixed to its upper torso was a pair of huge, leather-like appendages—wings, in other words—of a distinctly bat-like nature. As the headlights of his vehicle bathed the animal in a cascade of light, Perks could see that bones shone through its legs, which appeared practically hollow. But most terrifying of all was the head of the monster: Hairless and with two pointed ears, its fiery eyes burned deep into Perks's soul. A malevolent sneer broke out on its hook-nosed face while a pair of large, lethal-looking fangs extended down from a gaping mouth.

Perks had the presence of mind not to stop. In fact, he did precisely the opposite: He floored the accelerator and headed right for the beast. But like a chain-rattling spook from some 19th-century Gothic novel, it vanished in an instant. A shaken Perks made his way home and to the safety of his bed. For a week all was normal. But during the early hours of November 14, 2000, he was violently jolted from his slumber by the sight of the devilish beast again, this time looming right over his frozen-with-fear form. It suddenly lunged forward, grabbed his wrists, and boomed in words that Perks assured me were 100-percent accurate: "You were told that I would come."

Perks realized, in a terrifying instant, that this was the follow-up visit that Sarah Key had carefully and specifically warned him about. As Perks stared at the beast in stark terror, a telepathic message bellowed around his head. It was much the same as that of the Woman in Black: Stay away from all things Arthurian. And with that, the beast was suddenly gone. And, for a while at least, so was Perks's research.

Not long after meeting with Perks in 2001, I moved to the United States to live, and never again had the opportunity to speak with him in person. Perks *did*, however, in the summer of 2008, quietly share some additional thoughts on the matter with several former members of the now-defunct British-based Staffordshire UFO Group.

By then, some seven years after I had met him, Perks had come to a most unusual conclusion: that Sarah Key and the horrific monster were, incredibly, one and the same. Key, in Perks's mind, was a shape-shifter who had ingeniously adopted the guise of a sleek and sultry representative of the British government as a means to silence Perks via a potent cocktail of intimidation and fear. But, when that approach failed, she let her feminine façade drop and presented herself in all her terrible glory. Like a junkie in search of the next fix, however, Perks just could not keep away from the quest to find the truth behind the tales of King Arthur for long, and he finally returned to the thrill of the chase. Until, that is, his life was tragically cut short by a massive heart attack on England's Salisbury Plain in the early spring of 2009.

Whether Perks's death was due to years of bad living, stress, and cigarettes, which he chain-smoked throughout my meeting with him, or the malevolent hand of the supernatural Sarah Key, the definitive Woman in Black, we will never know. But this is not the only occasion upon which cold, black beauty and a terrible winged beast have crossed paths. In a celebrated case from decades earlier, and from the other side of the world, they were actually fused into one.

It was a warm summer's evening in 1969, and Earl Morrison, a private with the U.S. Marine Corps, was stationed in Vietnam, sitting with two friends atop a bunker situated near Da Nang, a port city on the coast of the South China Sea at the mouth of the Han River. For reasons that Morrison and his friends could never really fathom, they all looked up, nearly simultaneously, and, to their astonishment, saw a strange figure crossing the night sky—and it was slowly coming in their direction.

"We saw what looked like wings, like a bat's, only it was gigantic compared to what a regular bat would be. After it got close enough so we could see what it was, it looked like a woman" (Worley 1972).

The winged woman, added Morrison, was entirely jet-black in color, but seemed to have a greenish glow about her. As she closed in on the dumbstruck trio and passed over them at a height of barely 6 feet (1.8 m), they could hear the distinct flapping of wings. Too astonished to do anything but sit in silence and awe, Morrison and his comrades simply stared for three or four minutes until the flying woman finally vanished into the darkness of the Vietnamese skies.

Could this strange, winged life form perhaps have been the diabolical Sarah Key, heading off on an earlier mission, on the other side of the world, to silence someone who was getting perilously close to a dark, ancient truth that had to

> *remain hidden at all costs? Unfortunately, in the*
> *case of Sarah Key and the Vietnamese Woman in*
> *Black, we have far more questions than we do sat-*
> *isfactory answers. Maybe that's precisely how the*
> *Men in Black, and the Women in Black, want it.*

There is yet another case involving a flying monster and a Woman in Black, and, on this occasion, a Man in Black as well. As with the terrifying experience of Colin Perks, it also dates from 2000.

For years, sinister and sensational stories have surfaced from the forests and lowlands of Puerto Rico that tell of a strange and lethal creature roaming the landscape by night and day, striking terror into the hearts of the populace. It has a pair of glowing red eyes, powerful, claw-like hands, razor-sharp teeth, a body not unlike that of a monkey, a row of vicious spikes running down the length of its back, and, occasionally, a pair of large and leathery bat-like wings. The beast is said to feed on the blood of the local animal—predominantly goat—population, after puncturing their jugular veins with two sharp teeth. That's correct: Puerto Rico has a monstrous vampire in its midst. Its name is the Chupacabra, a Latin term meaning "goat sucker."

Theories abound with respect to the nature of the beast, with some researchers and witnesses suggesting that the monster is some form of giant bat; others prefer the theory that it has extraterrestrial origins: The most bizarre idea postulated is that the Chupacabra is the creation of a top-secret genetic research laboratory hidden deep within Puerto Rico's El Yunque rainforest, located in the Sierra de Luquillo, approximately 25 miles (40 km) southeast of the city of San Juan.

On several occasions, I have traveled to the island of Puerto Rico to seek out the vampire-like Chupacabra for myself, and perhaps one day determine its true nature. On one particular occasion, while roaming around Puerto Rico in 2005 with Canadian filmmaker Paul Kimball (we were there to make a documentary titled *Fields of Fear*), I had the very good fortune to meet and interview a man named Antonio, a pig farmer who had an unusual experience in 2000 that led to a decidedly strange visit from a Woman in Black/Man in Black duo. As Antonio told me, one of his animals had been killed, after darkness had fallen, by the now-familiar puncture marks to the neck. In this case, however, the animal exhibited *three* such marks, rather than the usual two. In addition, a number of rabbits kept on the property had been slaughtered in an identical fashion.

At the time all of the carnage was taking place, a considerable commotion was being made by the rest of Antonio's animals. Upon hearing this, he rushed wildly out of his house with a machete in his hand, and flung it hard in the direction of the marauding predator. Strangely, he told me, the weapon seemed to bounce off something that seemed metallic in nature. In fact, Antonio suggested that what the machete had made contact with seemed armor-plated. Due to the overwhelming darkness, however, he had no idea what the creature may have been. But *something* deadly was most certainly prowling around the property. The most confounding aspect of the affair was still to come, however. That's right: Antonio was about to get a visit of the type we have encountered time and again in these pages.

Shortly after the killing of the pig and the rabbits, a man and a woman dressed in typical, official-looking black regalia (on a stifling hot day, no less), who announced they worked for NASA, arrived at the farm and quickly proceeded to ask Antonio a wealth of questions about what had occurred, what he had seen, and the way in which his animals had met their grisly fates. When the conversation was over, the pair thanked the bemused farmer, in a fashion befitting both the Women in Black and the Men in Black—wholly unemotionally, in other words—and left without uttering another word. How the dark duo even knew that the attacks had taken place, and why on earth NASA would be dispatching personnel to his farm to investigate them, Antonio had no idea at all.

One thing that Antonio told me he had held back from informing his two mysterious visitors was this: On the morning after the attack he found strange footprints on his property that were spread quite a distance from each other. He formed the opinion that whatever had made them had the ability to leap considerable distances, in a fashion similar to that of a kangaroo—or, perhaps, he mused, it had the ability to fly.

Leaping or flying monsters, Men and Women in Black, and mutilated animals collectively suggested that something highly strange was, and perhaps still is, afoot in Puerto Rico.

PART II:

The Theories

Hallucinations

Having now studied an abundance of data on encounters of the MIB kind, surely the most important questions of all are: Who—or what—are the Men in Black? And what is the true nature of their dark and unearthly agenda? Trying to answer those questions is a formidable task indeed; however, the veil of secrecy, darkness, and elusiveness that surrounds the MIB can be successfully penetrated and interpreted—if, that is, one possesses an understanding of the strange realms into which one should go snooping.

To even have a hope of understanding the complexities of the Men in Black phenomenon, we have to first take a deep look at the "three men" of MIB legend. Based on what you have read thus far, you may be forgiven for assuming that the trio I refer to are those sinister souls that have so often manifested out of places unknown to threaten, intimidate, and silence those who, by accident or design, dare to enter the ufological playpen. The three men I have in mind are *not* our mysterious visitors, however. No; they are a trio of other, very different characters. And in many ways they are even more mysterious and legendary than the Men in Black themselves. Indeed, without these particular three men, the phenomena of the MIB would simply not exist—or, at least, it would not exist in the form and motif in which it is today most readily recognized. The three men to whom I refer are—if you have not yet fully surmised—Albert Bender, Gray Barker, and John Keel.

It is only by trying to understand the inner workings of this band of story-weavers extraordinaire that we can make at least some sense of the Men in Black. And to do so, it is essential that we examine the thoughts, ideas, conclusions, and memories of various key figures in ufology who met, knew, or corresponded with the three, who have studied their lives, experiences, and careers deeply. We start, as we surely must, with Albert Bender.

Many students of ufology are content to dismiss Bender's story without even a second thought, particularly the admittedly hard-to-believe tales of his wild trip to Antarctica, and his clams of having been entrusted with the alleged truth behind the UFO phenomenon. Jerome Clark, one of the most learned and clear-headed thinkers in ufology, says, *"Flying Saucers and the Three Men* is, obviously, a mediocre science fiction novel. Bender, I'm sure, wrote it to get saucer buffs off his back. Even Barker was privately disappointed with the manuscript, as he told me a few years after its publication."

Nevertheless, Clark does not *totally* write off Bender as a fantasy-prone character of no consequence. As was noted earlier in the pages of this book, Clark gives credence to the possibility that Bender was visited, in 1953, by agents of the FBI. He continues, on a related line of thinking

> There is some substance, however much it got exaggerated, to *They Knew Too Much About Flying Saucers*. Something frightened Bender, and to some degree that something intrigued Gray Barker, who wasn't quite so cynical in the early 1950s as he was to become. Barker, however, blew hot and cold in his private thoughts, some preserved in correspondence. He knew that Bender was of a frightened, paranoid nature and—beyond that—liked people to pay attention to him. These considerations led Barker to wonder if Bender hadn't expanded some small, genuine incident into something extraordinary and melodramatic. At other times Barker wondered if maybe something truly unusual had occurred. Of course, the doubts he entertained were not mentioned in his entertaining book.

Jim Moseley, Gray Barker's closest friend up until Barker's death, says of Bender: "I think his story was just silly and naïve, and don't know why anyone would have believed it. I never did. I think Gray Barker did for a while, and then he eventually realized that it was nonsense. I think Bender wanted to go out in a blaze of glory, which is better than to go quietly or slowly. There was nothing original or detailed about anything he said. This story about the Antarctic was just ridiculous. I think he quickly got bored or discouraged with flying saucers and wanted to go out with a bang instead of a whimper. He just decided to quit."

But is that really all there is to it? Maybe not. Here's where things get murky—and controversial.

Jerome Clark may be on-target in his suspicion that Bender really *was* interviewed by FBI agents back in the early 1950s—possibly as a result of the 1953 recommendations of the CIA's Robertson Panel—and then subsequently turned what might have been a fairly traumatic encounter with a trio of G-men into a complex tale of visitation by three far more disturbing alien-like Men in Black. But there are other aspects of Bender's story that cry out for scrutiny, and suggest that far more may have been afoot in that dark attic all those years ago.

We have to start with Bender's state of health—physical and psychological. As I have noted, the man was a character of near-infinite complexities. An obsessive-compulsive who was deathly afraid of cancer, deeply involved in occult matters, and spent the majority of his time hanging out in his stepfather's dimly lit attic, Bender was hardly what many people might describe as normal. That does not mean, however, that Bender was incapable of existing in the real world; he certainly was. He held down a regular job with the Acme Shear Company, today known as Acme United Corporation. He established a phenomenally successful UFO research group—albeit one that was not fated to last for long—and he even penned a book: *Flying Saucers and the Three Men*. And really, who among us is worthy of defining what it means to be normal?

As I noted early on in the pages of this book, Bender was plagued by pummeling migraines, suffered from dizzy spells and acute light-headedness, was constantly bothered by sulfur-like odors in his immediate environment, and was often forced to lie down in his attic bed when the migraine attacks, odors, and dizziness overwhelmed him—at which point he would either fall asleep or enter into what was clearly an altered state of perception, and the Men in Black would then invade, and intrude upon, his privacy and slumber. For those who might doubt that Bender was prone to falling into a strange state of mind and consciousness, consider the man's own words: "Often I would seem to drift off as if a cloud were carrying me into the inky, boundless depths of space" (Bender 1962).

Many of the symptoms that affected Bender are quite explainable as something far more down-to-earth than the Men in Black: epilepsy, a condition that causes seizures, and results from abnormal or excessive synchronous neuronal activity in the brain. Epilepsy is somewhat unique in that there are no less than 40 different types of the condition, which have varying symptoms and forms of treatment. Perhaps of relevance to the Bender saga is the phenomenon of "single partial seizures"—also known as Jacksonian epilepsy—which can result in the sufferer experiencing mild to moderate hallucinations, confusion and fear, lightheadedness but not outright unconsciousness, and strong, imaginary odors in the immediate vicinity. Some of those affected by such seizures have reported odors resembling burning rubber and sulfur—*exactly* as Albert Bender reported. This latter condition is known as Phantosmia, and is defined as the presence of a smell that has no real, external point of origin. Effects of seizures can also involve the feeling of leaving one's physical body, which may not be so different from Albert Bender's repeated experiences of journeying into the inky, boundless depths of space, as he imaginatively worded it.

That Bender was affected to a severe degree by migraines may be an important factor in his story, too: Approximately 15 percent of epileptics report migraines. And among the most curious side effects of migraines are: the perception of floating lights in the immediate vision, strange and strong odors, and distortions in the size and shape of objects. On this latter point, recall that in one of his more significant attic-based encounters, as well as being overwhelmed by a smell of sulfur, Bender saw in the room, a "large object of indefinable outline"—which sounds very much like a migraine-induced distortion of perception (Bender 1962).

But what of the curious poltergeist activity that Bender reported? Surely *that* cannot be connected to something as mundane as epilepsy, right? Perhaps it can: In 1958, a parapsychologist named William Roll introduced the term *recurrent spontaneous psychokinesis*, or RSPK. Roll came to believe that repeated neuronal discharges resulting in epileptic symptoms might actually provoke RSPK, which in turn could lead the patient to inadvertently generate poltergeist activity in his or her immediate vicinity. Roll, commenting on his controversial research and theories, said that he had examined the cases of 92 individuals with suspected RSPK, of whom more than 20 had symptoms that seemed strongly suggestive of epilepsy.

If the overpowering sulfur-like odors, poltergeist activity, vivid hallucinations, feelings of dread and confusion, a sense of bodily separation, and dizziness and light-headedness Bender experienced *were* all prompted by some undiagnosed condition of the brain, then how do we explain the story of his alleged trip to Antarctica? If not simply an outright fabrication, such a convoluted and intricate tale would clearly require someone to hallucinate in a fashion far beyond what one would expect in someone with epilepsy or another disorder. Still, certain facets of this aspect of Bender's story could have been borne out of his own highly complex subconscious. In fact, there are very good reasons for believing that this is *precisely* from where they were generated.

Bender—who comes across as a solitary character at the best of times—never made any mention of girl-friends in the mid- to late 1940s, or even at the dawning of the 1950s, when his 20s were by then almost behind him. All the trips to the Bridgeport cinema that Bender describes—even on carefree Saturday nights when he should surely have been letting his hair down with a girl or two—were made alone. Bender *did* refer, on one occasion, to holding a party in the attic for a bunch of work friends, and stated that when they saw his horror-themed room, "the girls in the party seemed to be quite shocked…and didn't stray far from their escorts" (Bender 1962). We can, perhaps, infer a great deal indeed from the fact that nowhere in this story does Bender make any kind of reference to *his* escort.

For a man in his 20s, and verging upon his 30s by the time he seriously immersed himself in the UFO arena, not to have had a girlfriend, or a wife, might strike many as being odd. Certainly, it would not have been a healthy situation for Bender, physically or mentally, sitting all alone in a dark attic on weeknights and a dark cinema on the weekends. Such isolation can wreak mental and physical havoc upon a person's well-being. Not only that, but it can manifest within the subconscious in surprising and vivid ways.

In the pages of his 1962 book, *Flying Saucers and the Three Men*, Bender revealed the details of a late-1953 incident following his decision to close down the International Flying Saucer Bureau. As usual, this encounter began with the smell of sulfur, and, lo and behold, his three Men in Black were once again quickly on the scene to transport Bender back to Antarctica. This time, however, it was a much different experience: Three space-women dressed in white outfits appeared and began to perform healing treatments.

The aliens then reassured Bender that this was all for his own good. Indeed, they asserted that the mysterious treatments "will make life better for you. There is one dreaded disease on your planet that all persons fear, and you will have no need to fear this once you have received this treatment" (Bender 1962). Logic suggests that the dreaded disease that all persons fear was almost certainly cancer. And, recall that Bender had, *long* before his UFO experiences even began, a wholly irrational fear of developing cancer, which easily befitted the illogical mindset of the classic hypochondriac.

What all this tells us about Bender is that he was very lonely, had a terror of developing cancer—conveniently lessened by a reassurance from the aliens that he will now be *forever* cancer-free—and longstanding anxieties about having been visited by agents of the

FBI adorned in black fedoras or homburgs. Those internal worries then collided in chaotic fashion, duly spilled out of Bender's subconscious, and fell right into the heart of a semi-awake, altered state borne out of an undiagnosed condition of the brain—hence the sulfur-like smells, the strange out-of-body sensations, and the blackouts that went along with integral parts of the story. Remember, too, that Bender had a cousin who, years before, had supposedly been visited by a Woman in Black. We cannot rule out the possibility that Bender (who was well aware of the story) subconsciously added aspects of *that* event to his own. And thus, as a result of this curious, and possibly even unique, chain of events were born the Men in Black.

Greg Bishop also suggests that Bender's experiences may have been entirely of his own making—although certainly not from a deliberately deceptive or deceitful perspective:

> I think that because Bender was so involved in the occult, maybe this played on his subconscious and he had the experience in kind of a hypnagogic, waking dream state. For me, that makes more sense than entities that actually came into his room. I think that the interaction between our minds and the UFO phenomenon is a lot more important than people realize… Bender may have had some kind of a real experience, but became fantasy prone to the point of delusion. It's more like a Walter Mitty character where the world's revolving around him and it's exciting.

Bishop's theory that some of Bender's experiences may have been hypnagogic ones is significant. *Hypnagogia* is a term that describes the stage between wakefulness and sleep—a stage in the sleep process that may be dominated by a wide variety of sensory experiences. For example, those in hypnagogic states have reported hearing voices ranging from barely audible whispers to wild screams. Others have heard random snatches of speech—largely nonsensical, but occasionally containing unusual, fictional names—and some have seen disembodied heads, or what appear to be fully formed entities in their bedroom. All of this typified Bender's experiences. Humming, roaring, hissing, rushing, and buzzing noises are also frequently reported by people experiencing hypnagogia.

Finally, whether due to hypnagogia, epilepsy, or some other condition, all the evidence points to Bender's encounters being definitively home-grown. If further evidence were needed to bolster this theory, we have it. In early 1954 Bender met Betty, the woman of his dreams, and the two were married on October 18 of that year. No one should be surprised to learn that from then on the women from the stars bid Bender farewell, as did the Men in Black.

The most significant statement on this matter comes from Gray Barker, who, in 1980, said of Bender to researcher and author Jerome Clark, long after the Bender story had become a part of UFO history: "If I'd been there in his room while he was in 'Antarctica' maybe I would have seen him lying in his bed in a trance" (Randles 1997).

Let us now learn more about the remaining two characters that were as instrumental in generating and nurturing the Men in Black legend as was Albert Bender: Gray Barker and John Keel.

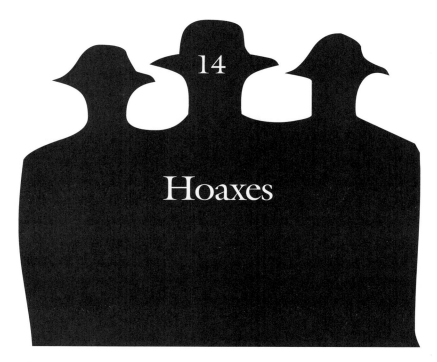

Hoaxes

Although the story of the Men in Black was most certainly that of Albert Bender, it would surely *never* have achieved the status and legend that it did without the input of Gray Barker. After all, it was Barker's 1956 book, *They Knew Too Much About Flying Saucers*, that really gave the saga widespread publicity— within the UFO research community and beyond it. Remember too that J. Edgar Hoover himself—the head honcho of the FBI—was moved to obtain a copy of the book in 1958. And it was Barker who published Bender's title, *Flying Saucers and the Three Men*, in 1962. Barker, then, was just as important in the development of the MIB mystery as was Bender—and, in terms of providing the story a great deal of public visibility, undoubtedly even more so. Moreover, Barker's written words had a profound impact on some of those individuals attracted to the UFO phenomenon in general and the Men in Black in particular, including Timothy Green Beckley, who says,

155

"My involvement with the Men in Black started when I was in the third grade. I had to do a book review, and most kids would probably do something like *A Tale of Two Cities* or a *Hardy Boys* book. I picked Barker's book, *They Knew Too Much About Flying Saucers*. I got a B+ on the review. I was mesmerized by the book and by the Men in Black silencing. It was very sinister to me, and has always had a great impression on me."

Moving on to John Keel, Beckley says, "I first met John at one of Jim Moseley's meetings. Jim used to have meetings here in Manhattan in the Hotel Woodstock and the Hotel Iroquois. Some of the meetings would attract small numbers of people—12 or 13—and sometimes as many as two or three hundred people. Keel popped up one night, and came in with Mary Hyre, the reporter from Point Pleasant who had seen the Men in Black. This was mid-'60s, and it turned out that John lived in my neighborhood." As both men were night owls, the young Beckley often went over to Keel's apartment in the late hours and hung out, listening to Keel entertain him with fantastic stories about "what had happened down in West Virginia with the strange phone calls, the Men in Black, and the Mothman sightings. Keel told me about how he was run off the road once, and was being followed. At first, I thought, "This guy has got a really great sense of imagination and is just trying to entertain me." But the more I got into the Men in Black stuff, the more I realized he was quite sincere about it all."

Allen Greenfield, who photographed a Man in Black in 1969, has crucial data to impart that gets to the heart of the nature of Barker and Keel, whom he describes as being, albeit in very different ways, "two of the most complex human beings I have ever met. And I'm very broadly traveled and have met a lot of unusual people. The fact that they covered some of the same territory should not confuse anyone that they should be approached in the same way. They shouldn't, at all."

Greenfield expands on this statement with respect to Keel: "He was a reporter. Now, he *was* a sensationalistic reporter; he would write stories for men's magazines back in the day. That was the genre he worked in for a very long time." Greenfield also notes, "There was, shall we say, some definite poetic license in Keel's writing. But he was an absolutely fascinating individual to sit down and talk with, and he had a spellbinding voice. I would not refer to him as a friend; he actually gave me the creeps. If he had put on a black suit and come to my door, I certainly would have thought: *this is one of the Men in Black.*"

Perhaps even Keel recognized that in the right circumstances he could very well pass for a mean Man in Black himself: In the opening pages of *The Mothman Prophecies*, for example, he related how, on a research trip to West Virginia in November 1967, while dressed *completely* in black, he was mistaken for a devilish entity by a couple whom he was forced to wake up and ask for help in the early hours of a stormy morning after his car had broken down near their home.

Greenfield makes an important distinction between Keel and Barker, with regard to the way they approached their respective investigations into Men in

Black cases: "Keel got the facts a lot better than Barker on cases they were both looking at. But Keel was far more credulous, and also more easily fooled, because, in a sense, he was outside of it all. Keel wasn't a ufologist; he was an observer of ufology. And that's a *very* different thing."

As for Barker, Greenfield offers the following thought-provoking words:

> Barker was a part of the phenomenon—that's what a lot of people miss when they ask, "Was he a hoaxer?" *Yes*, he *was* a hoaxer at times. Was he a fraud? No, absolutely not; he was *not* a fraud. He was a teller of folk tales, which can also be very truthful. And, to know Gray was to know the phenomenon. He told about realities, but he told them as stories. That was the culture he lived in.
>
> Asking whether Gray Barker was a truthful, honest person is like asking if Homer was a historian. It's a non-question; it's completely misunderstanding what one is dealing with. Gray was as much a part of the phenomenon as Kenneth Arnold's flying saucers. It was not reportage; he was telling the story, not attempting to come up with a pseudo-scientific explanation. And he could slip over into parable and metaphor, which was more about truth than a simple recitation of facts would ever be. All of that is the art of interpreting Gray Barker.

Perfectly demonstrating that Barker's involvement in ufology went way beyond merely chronicling hard facts, Jim Moseley admits, "Me and Barker pulled a couple of UFO hoaxes, and, I think, Barker pulled some hoaxes on Keel in the Point Pleasant context too. The funny thing is that Keel *liked* Barker, but he *hated* me. But, Barker and me, we were pretty much from the same camp and close friends."

Moseley reveals the details of one such cosmic caper: "There was one hoax where me and Barker took motion-picture of a UFO, which was about 30 or 40 seconds of film that I used in my lectures when I went on the college circuit. This was really just a little toy saucer that was dangled out the window of the car. I was driving the car, Barker was dangling it out the window, and a third guy, who was a friend of his, was on the roof of the moving car taking film of it. So, you've got all this different motion that looked fairly realistic. This would have been about 1966."

Faked UFO incidents aside, Moseley stresses that, as far as his written output was concerned, Barker wasn't a hoaxer, but he did have his own, unique style of telling a story that confounded and confused some of his readers: "Those cases he wrote about *did* happen, but they have been misconstrued, sometimes deliberately even by Gray, in order to make it a good story. But that's all. Gray could tell a great story by using his imagination, but *still* based on the facts. The truth is in his stories, but it's the way he presented it, as stories, that a lot of people don't always get."

Greg Bishop, who corresponded with Keel and met with him in New York City in 2001, echoes the words of both Moseley and Greenfield when it comes to trying to understand and dissect the nature of Barker: "It's obvious if you talk to Moseley, and look at some of Barker's writings, that he did have a genuine interest in the UFO subject, and thought there was a real mystery. He was also willing to bend the facts. But, that doesn't mean that the Bender story had nothing to it. It's the genesis of the whole Men in Black thing. It's the archetypal MIB story— as it relates to UFOs in the latter part of the 20th century. Barker, through Bender's story, created that mythos."

UFO authority Greg Bishop with John Keel, author of the acclaimed book *The Mothman Prophecies*.

When it comes to unraveling Keel, Bishop says, "His influence is *incredibly* huge, and the influence, I think, is mainly in his ideas, which were backed up by years and years of actually talking with people. That being said, he—like Barker—was not above bending some facts, or even making some up. But that doesn't bother me because it was his *ideas* that count: taking people, shaking them out, and pushing them in a new direction just by the sheer force of his writing and his storytelling."

Bishop offers the following as his parting words on Keel: "A nonfiction writer can be a great storyteller too, and Keel was one of the best at doing that. He was a Gonzo-Fortean, he was a trickster, and he knew it too. But he wasn't hoaxing—his fact-bending had a purpose: He was doing what he had to do to get a message and a theory across that he absolutely believed."

Jerome Clark has his own take on Barker and Keel:

Barker started out as a serious figure, but relatively early realized that he was never going to solve the mystery so he might as well have fun with it, thus all the exploitations and even outright hoaxes. Only he would have known what he really believed. From my conversations with him, I had the impression that his views were not unlike John Keel's, except that unlike Keel he felt no need or desire to reflect on it with any degree of concentration. And yes, he was a magnificent storyteller.

As for Keel, I think—I know, because he was sending field reports to me in the late 1960s—that he came upon genuine weirdness and reported on it generally accurately. As you well know, it's not hard to find weirdness if you go looking for it. Unfortunately, Keel insisted upon laying his crazy interpretations on all this material. He had a medieval mind and, worse, a cracked one. At his very best moments Keel's contribution to ufology and anomalistics was a decidedly mixed one. Mostly, he was a textbook example of a crank. I am sure, more to the point, that Barker was playing phone pranks on Keel; maybe other hoaxes too. That wasn't because Barker was a *Walter Mitty* type, however. He was a trickster who enjoyed putting one over on anyone who might be receptive, and Keel was receptive. His paranoia made him quite gullible.

Someone else who became acquainted with Keel when Men in Black activity was at its height in the 1960s was acclaimed paranormal authority Brad Steiger, whose astonishing words may help to clarify why Keel was so intrigued by the mystery of the MIB: "Sometime in 1966, [when] I was in New York working on my book *Valentino*, I visited Ivan T. Sanderson at his farm in New Jersey, then, later, called John Keel, who had said, 'When you're in town give me a call.' He took me to my first Chinese restaurant, and we had a delightful evening. And then we went back to his apartment, whereupon he began to alter my reality when he began telling me stories about researching Mothman and his encounters with the Men in Black."

And this is where things proceeded to get very, *very* strange. His voice dropping ever so slightly, but certainly noticeably, in tone, Steiger said to me, "I've *never* put this in *any* of my books, and I feel a little awkward, but on the other hand, what I am about to tell you really happened. John was a good-sized fellow and I couldn't see how just anyone could frighten him; and, at that time, I was 30 years old, in good shape, bench-pressing 450 pounds (204 kg). I was like, 'Bring it on! I'm not afraid of any Men in Black!' Then he began to tell me of the visitations he'd had with three men who had not knocked, but had entered, his apartment. They literally came *through* the door. He told me of an evening when they were challenging him to lay off the whole Mothman thing; to lay off UFOs, if he knew what was good for him."

Having heard that astounding aspect of the story—which sounds astonishingly like Albert Bender's experiences with the three MIB that materialized in his attic—you might think, "Could it get any stranger?" Yes, it could, and it certainly does. Back to Steiger:

> John was the sort of person who responded to threats like the red flag to the bull. But, he said to me that, on this occasion, [the MIB] reached under his sink and took out a jug of Clorox. They asked, "What is this?" and John said, "That's disinfectant; it's very powerful." They brought it over to him, took the cap off, and gave him a smell. John wrinkled his nose, and when they asked if it was Clorox, he said, "Yes, that's what it is. Now put it back before you spill it." Whereupon the three of them—in front of him—put it to their lips one at a time and took large gulps of it. Now, by the time John had finished the evening, telling me stories like this, I decided that maybe I wouldn't be quite so brave and quite so powerful. I began thinking, "We're not dealing with FBI agents or the Air Force."

Then there are the memorable words of Colin Bennett, a firsthand witness to a Man in Black in the early 1980s: "Barker may indeed have written episodes of supposed UFO history himself just to keep the narrative going, or kick-start it when it lagged. But skeptics, foaming at the mouth, should be warned here that this is not witness to their claims of the falsehood of all ufological experience. Story-breeders may fulfill precisely the object of contact: not only will they tell the story, they will expand it, adding episodes of their own in order to try and initiate mythological change and development.... Such mimetic game-play operates on the recognized principle that when we *imagine* we create a form of life."

What we can ascertain from the combined words of Greenfield, Beckley, Steiger, Moseley, Bishop, Bennett, and Clark is that one must be very careful how one interprets the published words of both Barker and Keel. And one must also note that this mighty duo had no qualms about turning a fairly good story into an atmospheric and Gothic one—a bright, sunny day becomes the proverbial dark and stormy night. They were not, however, simply concocting stories from their collective imaginations. Rather, they were telling fantastic truths, albeit in somewhat distorted, imaginative, literary fashions. The reason? To provoke new thought, ideas, and paradigms.

Thus, the Men in Black certainly live, but perhaps our idea of them as derived from the works of Barker and Keel should be viewed through careful filters.

We may now have somewhat of an understanding of the complex players and chain of events that led to the early formation of the MIB legend. This same legend, however, cannot, under any conventional circumstances, explain the myriad encounters with the Men in Black that followed—and that *continue* to follow—in the dark wake of Bender's hallucinogenic experiences. There may, however, be an explanation for this conundrum. And it's an explanation that takes us on a wild ride into some truly fantastic realms of possibility.

The imagery provoked by Bender's three Men in Black and the tales of their visits and threats were, and still are, undeniably powerful and emotive ones. And, much like a modern-day meme, such imagery quickly spread throughout the UFO research community, eventually reaching the U.S. government, J. Edgar Hoover, the military, the media, and the world of Hollywood. These undeniably powerful motifs, born of Bender and elaborated upon by the story telling techniques of Barker and Keel, and subsequently instilled in the minds of thousands of people, may have inadvertently led to the creation of a whole new breed of Men in Black that extended far beyond anything Bender and Barker could have dreamed of back in the early 1950s. It is the breed of the Tulpa. And if you don't have an understanding of the nature of the Tulpa, you are now about to.

Tulpas and Vampires

"The Men in Black tend to seem badly briefed," Chris O'Brien suggests. "It's like they manifest for a particular task, and they know what they're supposed to do and what they're supposed to say, but they exist in a framework of having no context. In other words, they are almost like manifested beings, or manufactured, temporary entities that don't seem to have any sort of depth to them."

He continues, "The $64,000,000 question is, Who's behind this? The Men in Black may be some sort of collective manifestation. I think there may be some sort of symbiotic relationship between the phenomena and people's expectations of how it's going to appear. And they're very cliché, too—*very* cliché—which tends to support the idea that we, or something, are manifesting these entities. It's almost like they're Tulpas."

And what, you may be asking, are Tulpas? To answer that complex question, we first need to focus our

167

attentions upon a certain Alexandra David-Neel. Born Louise Eugenie Alexandrine Marie David in France on October 24, 1868, David-Neel was the first woman ever to be granted the prestigious title of Lama in Tibet. Throughout her century-long life, David-Neel—who was both an anarchist and a Buddhist—traveled widely across Asia, had a deep love for the Himalayas, and, in 1932, penned a fascinating book about her many and varied adventures titled *Magic and Mystery in Tibet*. It is, in many ways, due to David-Neel that the phenomenon of the Tulpa has come to be known and appreciated outside of Tibetan teachings and culture.

The word *Tulpa* can be traced directly back to the Tibetan language and refers specifically to an entity, or a being, that attains some form of meaningful reality after being conjured up solely from the imagination of the conjurer. The process of creation is a complex one and requires an immense amount of skill and dedication, but those carefully trained in the ancient art of the Tulpa can draw the imagery out of the confines of their minds and into the world of the physical.

David-Neel, it transpires, had become fascinated and obsessed by the lure, mystery, and potential of the Tulpa—to the point at which she ultimately elected to try to create one for herself. In David-Neel's case, she chose to visualize the image of an overweight, genial monk—perhaps not unlike the Friar Tuck character in Hollywood Robin Hood films. The process of trying to create the image of the monk was both time-consuming and draining, but, after a while, David-Neel was finally able to see her ethereal monk not only in her mind but also in the real world. In other words, a brand-new kind of spectral life form was coming into being.

In time, the vision of the monk grew in clarity and substance until it was completely indistinguishable from physical reality, as David-Neel said: "He became a kind of guest, living in my apartment. I then broke my seclusion and started for a tour, with my servants and tents. The monk included himself in the party. Though I lived in the open riding on horseback for miles each day, the illusion persisted. It was not necessary for me to think of him to make him appear. The phantom performed various actions of the kind that are natural to travelers and that I had not commanded. For instance, he walked, stopped, looked around him. The illusion was mostly visual, but sometimes I felt as if a robe was lightly rubbing against me, and once a hand seemed to touch my shoulder" (David-Neel 1971).

But, rather like rebellious teenagers tired of Mom and Dad telling them what to do and what not to do, the day finally came when the manufactured monk slipped from David-Neel's conscious control. Even worse: Its genial character began to morph in both its attitude and appearance. David-Neel was now entering truly dangerous and, for her, previously uncharted territory. In her own words: "The fat, chubby-cheeked fellow grew leaner, his face assumed a vaguely mocking, sly, malignant look. He became more troublesome and bold. In brief, he escaped my control" (David-Neel 1971).

At this crucial juncture, David-Neel concluded that things had gone much too far, and she began to apply a variety of ancient techniques of Lamaism to try and reabsorb the now-malevolent creature back into the depths of her own mind. Not surprisingly, the Tulpa was most unwilling to face personal obliteration. Fortunately, however,

David-Neel finally succeeded, after a horrendous period of more than six months, during which time the mind-monk grew ever more vicious, spiteful, and filled with hate for its creator, as it struggled—ultimately in vain—to prevent David-Neel from ending its "life."

How can such a creature of the imagination break free of its mind-based moorings, rather than only surfacing when the creator wishes it to appear? A Tulpa, David-Neel was told by Tibetan occultists, begins to act independently when it is endowed with sufficient vitality and energy to take on some semblance of physical reality. She was further informed that this is an almost inevitable part of the overall process and is not at all unlike the natural birthing process that occurs between mother and child. Tibetan magicians had also informed David-Neel of cases involving Tulpas that had been dispatched to fulfill specific missions or tasks, but subsequently failed to do so, and instead began following their own dangerously mischievous agendas. If the creator of the Tulpa should pass away before the deconstruction process is completed, David-Neel was warned, it will do its utmost to cling to its life. And if left unchecked it stands a very good chance of thriving.

Alexandra David-Neel, however, was not the only person of significance to have brought—recklessly so, and without any meaningful forethought, one might say—Tulpas into our world from the depths of her mind.

Born in 1873, Franek Kluski, whose real name was Teofil Modrzejewski, had a long history of paranormal experiences that began in childhood. He recalled, for example, seeing dead relatives, long-deceased pets, and other phantom animals. But it was not until 1918, after a séance, that Kluski's mediumistic potential was finally recognized, and a series of truly mind-blowing séances began in earnest. Indeed, Kluski's reputation was such that the number of those attending his sittings very soon ran into the hundreds and included a host of people from all walks of society.

Most intriguing were the materializations that occurred during Kluski's séances. These included a huge dog, a spectral bird, a giant cat that resembled a lion, and a large ape-like creature (many of which parallel the unidentified entities seen in England's Cannock Chase woods referred to in the Introduction). According to Gustave Geley, MD, who participated in Kluski's séances at the Paris Institut Metapsychique International, "All these phantoms give the impression of being alive" (Barrington 1993). Notably, these quasi-real creatures also materialized in front of Kluski in his own abode on occasions when he was not performing his séances. In other words, the giant cat, the phantom dog, and the spectral monkey-beast eventually took on independent existences—just as had Alexandra David-Neel's chubby monk.

But how do the entities that manifested before Franek Kluski and the maniacal monk that Alexandra David-Kneel created thrive in our own environment? The answer is twofold, and is as terrifying as it is simple: The very fact that we believe in the Tulpa assists its ability to maintain a significant foothold in our reality. And, whereas we feed on animals, fruits, and vegetables, they feed on elevated states of human emotion. How do they achieve that ability to feed? They deliberately go out of their way to provoke emotional states.

Could it be that Albert Bender's personal terror about the Men in Black and Gray Barker's ability to vividly portray their actions led to such a strong belief in (and acceptance of) the MIB that they strode right out of the minds of Bender and Barker and into the real world, in the form of Tulpas? To answer this, let's take a careful look at what we know about the Men in Black.

The Tulpa thrives on high states of emotion. In the case of the Men in Black, that high state of emotion would be pure fear. This, one could argue, would perhaps explain why the MIB are always careful to ensure they instill terror in witnesses of UFO activity—even when the case itself may not be of any high degree of significance or importance. In other words, it is the fear-drenched response of the witness—rather than the actual intricacies of the UFO encounter itself—that is of vital importance to the Men in Black. It is this, more than anything else, that dictates their actions and sustains their existence in our world.

Timothy Green Beckley makes a valuable observation about this issue: "The weird thing about the Men in Black is that they sometimes take an interest in the most mundane cases where, if it wasn't for the presence of the Men in Black, no one would care about the sightings themselves. So, that's odd: They draw attention to themselves by frightening and silencing people whose sightings aren't really that special at all. They just seem to pick witnesses at random, sometimes."

Maybe that randomness is not quite so random, after all. Maybe the MIB are driven by the one thing that defines us: the need for self-preservation. Perhaps, when the actions of the Men in Black are less widely reported within UFO publications and the mainstream media, belief in their existence and the attendant emotional response to their presence begin to diminish. And as that belief shrinks to the point at which they are seen as little more than hoaxes, myths, and legends, their power and presence in our environment diminishes also. Thus, they become little more than specters without true form or identity. This may also go some way toward explaining why, on occasion, the Men in Black barely seem self-aware, and behave in such odd fashions. Maybe, as their lives begin to fragment and disintegrate around them, they literally start to lose their minds.

Perhaps this is why Men in Black activity seems to occur in cycles and waves, such as at Point Pleasant, West Virginia, in the 1960s: The MIB actively seek out UFO witnesses to ensure strong emotional feedings. And as the MIB then feed upon the emotions of the witnesses, their ability to operate and be seen in our world in full physical form is extended. Inevitably this added opportunity for them to coexist with us physically, and for a longer period of time, means a greater likelihood of being spotted by others, who then also fall victim to their visits. By this process, the MIB gain even more emotional strength.

Thus a cycle is created wherein one MIB sighting leads to another, and belief in their existence is bolstered via the media and word of mouth. The Men in Black then secure an ever-increasing foothold in our world as emotions run high, sightings escalate, and the energy-based food supply of the MIB grows. But then, they suddenly vanish as enigmatically as they first appeared. Why? The answer may be very simple: They are now fully fueled and sated. And like an animal in the wild, they will only seek out fresh, new prey when hunger, and a dire need to ensure their curious form of life continues, begins to overtake them once again.

Perhaps occasionally the refueling process fails to work, such as in the 1976 case of Dr. Herbert Hopkins, when the energy of his Man in Black plummeted to the levels one might expect to see in a diabetic in need of an emergency sugar fix. Perhaps Hopkins's visitor, unable to suck the emotion out of Hopkins for reasons beyond our comprehension, headed off into the dark night to taunt and feed upon another unfortunate player in the world of the UFO.

There is another interesting bit of information to be gained from Dr. Hopkins's visitation: It was specifically his *invitation* that led the Man in Black to darken his door and enter the family home. I am reminded here of the old folklore concerning the way the legendary vampire can only enter one's home when it receives permission to do so. The vampires of centuries past were also predatory life forms that derived sustenance from humanity—albeit in the form of blood. Remember, too, that, in England in 2000, Colin Perks's Woman in Black stood in silence on his doorstep, specifically awaiting permission to enter his home.

I have to wonder, therefore: Could some of those old legends of blood-sucking beings feeding upon us have actually been distortions of real-life encounters with proto-MIB characters in centuries past, whose sole mission was to secure vital nourishment from us? After all, is there really very much difference between a black-cloaked, pale-faced vampire craving our blood, and a black-suited, white-as-a-sheet Man in Black voraciously hungry for our emotions? I would strongly suggest not. Perhaps, therefore, Albert Bender only gave birth to *modern-day*, Tulpa-style Men in Black. Maybe, in centuries past, there were many others like Bender who also inadvertently—or maybe deliberately—opened the doors of their subconscious and unleashed similar imagery into the real world.

Lest you think I am the only one who has suggested such a theory with respect to the Men in Black, consider the words of Allen Greenfield: "The thing about the cases that Keel, Barker, and a number of others were most interested in is that these Men in Black don't seem to be human beings at all. They seem like they have to make an effort to appear human. It's like they're trying to project their existence from moment to moment, and having a lot of trouble doing it." He continues, "In some cases, people feel like the Men in Black have sucked energy out of the air, so you have vampire comparisons—psi-vampires. Whatever they are, they seem to draw their energy from the environment around them."

Continuing on this line of thought, Greenfield says,

Maybe the Men in Black are generated by fear. I have a hunch that fear may be a major factor in generating a good deal of the phenomenon of UFOs in general. Although there seems to be some separate intelligence that is involved too. I don't think it's all generated, pure and simple, by the witnesses. It seems to me there is a kind of … panic that is the ingredient that produces, or predicts, the manifestation of the coming of the fear-inducing beings. And that would range from the Men in Black and their threats to the alien abduction phenomenon.

Greenfield's words are equally relevant to the stories of Albert Bender that contained strong themes of both terror and space-girl eroticism. Greenfield offers the following with regard to the operations of the Men in Black, which also echoes my thoughts on the puzzle as it relates to the idea of Tulpas: "It seems that the whole experience causes fear to the witness, and I wonder if generating fear is the entire goal of the experience. If whatever the source of this is derives its energy from literally soaking up human fear, then the stronger the emotion, the stronger the fear. I would say it's almost certainly the case that when the Men in Black tell people not to talk about UFOs, that's *not* done to silence them."

So, what is the reason? Greenfield's theories are right in line with the notion that the MIB may be Tulpas: "It's done to scare them into this state of high emotion. The threat is a ruse to create this rush of fear and energy. And, ironically, the reverse is true about the Men in Black threats. People are told not to talk about what they've seen, but that actually sends them screaming and running to the police, their priest, or UFO groups. So, the response of the witness is usually the exact opposite of what the Men in Black are allegedly trying to achieve."

Greenfield's final words on this matter are memorable. Indeed, they're downright petrifying: "In some cases, it's like we're a source of food; they may be taking fear and, in simplistic terms, eating it."

Colin Bennett has also noted that the Men in Black seem to have very different lives from ours: "It appears fairly obvious to me that MIB are liminal manifestations as much as is Bigfoot. Like the UFO itself, the MIB and Bigfoot look like short media clips more than anything else. We can easily assume that any alien form may well have evolved into pure media, leaving behind mechanical traces perhaps millions of years ago. With such large animal cryptids as reported, there is no food swathe, no signs of nesting or breeding, no droppings, [no] signs of tribal fights, and—most important of all—no skeletal remains upon death, fatal injury, or illness."

"The Man in Black," Bennett continues, "differs of course from, say, Bigfoot, in that the Man in Black takes a humanoid form [and] has a limited language, and an equally limited presence. But similar to Bigfoot, our Man in Black has no social background. Every single one of these animal and humanoid cryptids appears to be a limited simulation possessing a very short half-life, rather like a collection of discarded film-edits. We have, therefore, a detectable program at work here whose limitations are functions of its own psychosocial and dialectical resolution. The edits are the key to the program."

Bennett turns his attention to his own Man in Black encounter in London in the early 1980s: "The quick exits and entrances of the MIB are a good defense, of course. In my case our visitor made sure that I didn't have time to form certain kinds of questions whose answers might reveal the absence of true, live, human biocomplexity. I think he was reading me as my questions were forming in my head, and he got out quick." He also notes, "We have to conclude therefore that our overspecialized, over-serious, predictable, and extremely limited Man in Black is capable only of producing very simple simulacra for a very short time."

As we draw to a close on this particular issue, it's worth noting that in a letter to John Keel, Gray Barker wrote, "There is a method which I have used which has kept me relatively unbothered by the MIB syndrome.... If the reader is ever confronted by one of these strange people...don't respond in fear. Most important, make some sort of joke! If you throw off their programming, they will be 'short-circuited,' so to speak, and will probably run screaming into the night or fade out like a motion picture would do" (Moseley 1967).

Colin Bennett says of Barker's words, "It sounds here as if Barker himself had had an MIB contact and had created a means of exorcising such things." It also sounds very much like Barker was keenly aware of the reasons why the Men in Black were so reliant on fear and why it was so important for the witness *not* to provide them with the nourishment they have coldly craved for so long. Perhaps Barker took with him to the grave deep suspicions about the origins of the MIB that, nearly 30 years after his early passing, we'll never know.

16

Tricksters

Connected to the Tulpa is the ancient phenomenon of the Trickster. Chris O'Brien, one of the most learned scholars on this often-misunderstood subject, says, "It's tough to define what the Trickster phenomenon is, but it's the oldest archetypal symbol within the collective human unconscious. That's why we have clowns; they do absurd things, and they're a holdover from the original primordial Tricksters. And you absolutely have that element of absurdity in the Men in Black thing."

O'Brien concludes that the main role of the Trickster is to supply anti-structure and novelty within the culture or subculture, and to topple the status quo. In doing so it allows culture to move forward and creates room for growth, instead of being rigidly stuck in one particular control system.

"And that," says O'Brien, "can be in the form of anthropomorphizing animals. And supplying technology

179

is one of the primary things that comes through all the Trickster stories around the world. Like the introduction of agriculture and fishing nets, different aspects of technological development in many stories are supplied by Trickster elements. So, it's not just one thing. It's collectively inherited unconscious ideas, patterns of thought, images, or ideas universally present in individual psyche. That is my own definition. The main view is that the Trickster is static, it does *not* evolve, it is unconscious, and it is *not* self-aware. But I have attempted to refute that. I think it *is* evolving, it is *not* static and it *is* becoming self-aware, but it remains amoral."

Turning his attention specifically to the Men in Black, O'Brien observes that there are some major correlations with the Trickster phenomenon: "We're dealing with individuals that *seem* to be sinister, but they're not. It's more of a *suggestion* about something that's sinister, and then the MIB visit seems to lend something sinister to the UFO encounter. The Men in Black have become almost an archetypal symbol. We're talking about something deeply rooted in our consciousness, starting with Barker and on to Keel. And I think these stories have gotten out to enough of a degree to actually create an archetypal figure in our collective consciousness. I think, with the MIB thing, it's an under-investigated and underappreciated element of the Trickster phenomenon."

Regan Lee has her own thoughts on the Trickster aspect of the Men in Black phenomenon: "One thing that strikes me about the Men in Black is that we have two concurrent ideas about who they are. There are the government agents, and then you have this other Men in Black phenomenon that goes way, way back—even centuries. So, I'm fascinated by these two different types, or timelines, of Men in Black. And although Men in Black are usually associated with UFOs, there are other stories that have little or nothing to do with UFOs—paranormal ones, where the MIB appear. Are they real entities? Could they be inter-dimensional?"

Lee is inclined to think they may be something similar to what we would call Djinn. The Djinn (from which the word *genie* is derived) have their origins in Arabian folklore and the teachings of Islam, and are shape-shifting Tricksters that can be benign, hostile, or entirely neutral in nature. They can also be deceptively manipulative just for the thrill of it. "They appear to mess with us," Lee says, "to interfere with us. Is this their idea of having fun? Maybe it's more insidious, or a little bit of all of that. It goes beyond the government spooks; although there's no doubt there are government spooks running around who may be pretending to be the real Men in Black. But the real Men in Black, they like to mess with us—like Tricksters. That's their idea of a good time: mess with the humans."

Another legendary Trickster is the fairy of ancient Celtic lore. In contrast to the modern-day friendly, welcoming imagery many people associate with fairies—as beautiful, winged entities of small stature—in centuries long gone, these beings were perceived as having the potential to be downright deadly, cause mayhem and disaster in the home, steal newborn babies and replace them with crudely formed wooden effigies (modern-day alien abductions and extraterrestrial/human hybrids, perhaps?), and hold deep, long-lasting grudges. You may ask, "So what does this particular brand of Trickster have to do with the Men in Black?" Read on....

"This is one of those stories that are purely anecdotal," says Regan Lee of a very curious early 1970s MIB event she has investigated. "It happened years ago; there's no evidence and certainly no proof. Dates and times are non-exact; witnesses, except for the one who shared the following with me, are not to be found. But there's one thing within this story that is very peculiar, as we'll see." The location was the Owens Valley in Eastern California, east of the Sierra Nevada mountains, on what was described by the witness as a "hippie commune." The area was remote, and as Lee notes, "No one wore a suit, if they even owned a suit. This detail is important" (Lee 2010).

The UFO sighting that invited the Men in Black to come calling was a typical one: Lee's friend, along with two other witnesses, was driving on a nearby highway at night, when they were all witness to a very large UFO in the night sky. It had "large white lights that went all around," as Lee's friend worded it. They watched the device in the sky above them for a few moments, until it zoomed off (Lee 2010). "My friend doesn't remember if they told anyone of the sighting," Lee adds, 'but [she] doesn't think they did. None of the witnesses thought to call any agency to report it; for one thing, they really had no idea who to call, and for another, this was in the early 1970s, and self-described hippies calling in a UFO sighting to an official agency just didn't occur to them" (Lee 2010).

Nevertheless, this lack of reportage didn't faze the Men in Black: They were soon on the scene. Only a couple of days after the encounter, two men appeared at the commune. At the time, Lee's friend was alone with her children; everyone else was gone, off to work or running errands. Lee says that her friend "described the men as wearing business suits, which struck her as extremely odd. No one in that area wore suits; the thought of men driving around in a remote area, in suits, was just plain weird. They showed her [some] ID, she's pretty sure, but doesn't remember what agency they said they were from. But she was a young woman, living a counter-culture lifestyle out in the middle of nowhere, and two official men in suits arrive at her door. Easy to see how she could be a little flustered and intimidated. She took their word that they were who they said they were" (Lee 2010).

The MIB quickly got to the point and began asking probing questions about her UFO encounter, which in itself was very curious, as she had chosen not to mention the incident to anyone. Then the questions became bizarre. The Men in Black wanted to know if she, or anyone else on the commune, had noticed anything different, or unusual, about the way "the milk from the animals" tasted.

"When I heard that, I knew I had something important, "Lee says. "I had never heard of that question being asked before in the context of UFO encounters, and my first thought was a connection between this sighting and cattle mutilations. I asked my friend if she was aware of any cattle mutilations in the area at the time; I'm not sure she understood what I was talking about exactly. But she agreed that was a very weird question to be asked" (Lee 2010).

When Lee shared this story with me in November 2010, I quickly realized that the line of questioning developed by the Men in Black might have had far *less* to do with cattle mutilations and far *more* to do with matters of a specifically Trickster nature. I told Lee in an e-mail, "Do a Google search on 'fairy + sour milk' and you'll see how the two go together. This could, perhaps, place these MIB in a definitively paranormal or Trickster realm. Within English folklore there is the legend of the Boggart—a malevolent entity that had a particular, unfathomable penchant for souring milk. Scotland has the equally milk-hating Bogle. And within Latvian culture we hear of the Lauma, a beautiful woman who steals babies and maliciously taints milk."

Take note of the following from John Keel: "The fairy lore of the Celtic countries is also filled with tales of Men in Black. In fact, part of the fairy belief includes fairies who are the size of normal men and who walk almost unnoticed among humans except for their black clothing. Like their smaller counterparts, they were said to be great mischief-makers" (Beckley 1990).

Lee adds, after reviewing the relevant data from fairy legend: "If we consider aliens and the UFO phenomena to be within this fairy realm of Trickster magick and the paranormal, along with the mythic veneration of the cow as a sacred being/deity, and government MIB as shadowy figures representing another realm, we see that [we are] definitely on to something. There are abundant clues in this context of the UFO phenomena, or at least some aspects of it, as transcending just nuts-and-bolts, aliens-from-another-planet explanation, and placing it in the paranormal realm" (Lee 2010).

Are the MIB Trickster-style entities who, for their own obscure reasons chose to upgrade an ancient motif straight out of the fairy world for a modern audience? Or are they government agents concerned about dastardly aliens poisoning the nation's supply of milk? Both scenarios sound bizarre in the extreme. Or perhaps *absurd* would be a more appropriate word.

Many years ago, Timothy Green Beckley was told by Gray Barker of an MIB encounter that occurred in Arko, Utah. The witness was a schoolboy, one Robert McCallister, who on the day at issue was roaming around his local woods when he stumbled upon a relatively small, circular-shaped device, hovering approximately 6 feet (1.8 m) off the ground in an isolated clearing. Suddenly three tall, unusual-looking men appeared—as did a silver-haired character, sitting atop a floating chair, no less—who invited McCallister for a tour of the compact flying saucer.

Intriguingly, just like one of Mary Hyre's several Men in Black that appeared at Point Pleasant, West Virginia, in the 1960s, the presumed alien seemed fascinated by a ball-point pen sticking out of McCallister's pocket, which the boy subsequently offered to the enigmatic figure as a gift. Seemingly very pleased—*far too pleased*, it might be argued—the man, in turn, gave McCallister a present of a small, black, plastic-like tube. Then McCallister was motioned to leave the craft and keep his distance—which he did—as it soon took to the skies and vanished. It was only later that McCallister realized the priceless artifact had mysteriously vanished from his pocket. Author Jacques Vallee explains the relevance in the fairy realm of this type of encounter: "...centuries-old folklore is replete with tales of people who claimed to have visited the realm of the fairies and who tried to bring back with them a souvenir, only to be thwarted, in one form or another, from doing so at the last minute" (Vallee 1970). Such experiences, in times past, often occurred in isolated clearings deep in the woods—just like that of McCallister.

But why was McCallister in the woods in the first place? He was laying traps to catch coyote. It so transpires that within Native American cultures the coyote is one of the most celebrated of all the many and varied Tricksters. A shape-shifter, a jester, a messenger, and more, the coyote is often a thief too. A ballpoint pen may not seem like much, but—just like Mary Hyre's Man in Black—McCallister's mysterious man seemed mighty happy indeed to get his hands on that little innocuous item. And, in the process, he ensured that, ultimately, his gift to McCallister vanished.

Also relevant to the Trickster angle of the MIB phenomenon is the experience of Peter Rojcewicz, who, in 1980, was confronted by a Man in Black in the library of the University of Pennsylvania, when he just happened to be researching for his PhD thesis in folklore. Out of the blue, and just as the library seemed curiously and ominously absent of anyone else, appeared a tall, thin man, demonstrating somewhat of a European accent, dressed in the now-familiar color. A conversation began that, given Rojcewicz's folkloric connections, hit upon UFOs. The man inquired of Rojcewicz if he thought UFOs were a reality, to which Rojcewicz offered that he was far more interested in such things from a folkloric perspective. This did not go over well at all. The Man in Black became irate, and stressed how significant the whole UFO phenomenon was. After Rojcewicz tried to calm the Man in Black, he simply placed a hand on Rojcewicz's shoulder, and suggested in curious words that Rojcewicz should go well in his purpose. That Rojcewicz—after meeting the strange Man in Black—ultimately went on to become a department chair and professor of humanities at the Juilliard School and a dean at the School of Holistic Studies at the John F. Kennedy University, is, perhaps, evidence of the way in which, as Chris O'Brien words it, the Trickster "allows culture to move forward, and creates room for growth."

There's still further evidence of Trickster-style shenanigans when it comes to the MIB. When I was close to concluding my interview with Jim Moseley about his views on Albert Bender's claims of being visited by the Men in Black in the early 1950s, Moseley practically shouted down the telephone to me: "This is funny... there's something wrong with the phone here! The longer I talk the more static I get!" Perhaps the souls of Barker and Keel decided to turn the tables, and duly partook in a few tricks from the other side on Moseley. Or maybe the Men in Black—so keen on playing disruptive games with our telephones—were engaging in a few Trickster-like shenanigans of their own. Given that Moseley is skeptical of much of the MIB lore, possibly, in their own unique way, the Tricksters were trying to tell him that he should not be quite so skeptical after all.

Colin Bennett has one last thing to say of his 1982 encounter with a Man in Black in a London apartment: "Here I have a confession to make. At this time, I had a play of mine being performed at the London Institute of

Contemporary Arts. The title of my play was 'All Along the Watchtowers' and it was about UFOs and Men in Black." That Bennett should have personally encountered a Man in Black at the same time that his stage production was in full swing is surely indicative of a Trickster's manipulation.

Raven Meindel's 2008 experience with the Men in Black also displays evidence of a Trickster's presence. Recall her words on what she was doing when her two MIB happened on the scene: "I was outside playing with a Frisbee with a neighborhood kid. The Frisbee was called an *Alien Flyer*, which had an alien face on it, which I thought was a *very* odd synchronicity."

Whatever the case, the joke is always on us. The key is to try and understand what the joker, or the Trickster, in its own oblique way, is telling us.

17

Civilian Investigators

Certainly not all Men in Black can be considered Tulpas or Tricksters. Evidence suggests that the overall phenomenon may have multiple, wildly varying origins. Let us now turn our attentions to one of the most obvious angles; namely, that *certain* cases are borne out of nothing stranger than misidentification. Although I do not personally believe that this can satisfactorily explain *all* the MIB cases presently on record—or even a large number of them—it may very well offer answers to a few incidents that have gained a degree of legendary status. Speaking of this aspect of the MIB puzzle, Jim Moseley says, "One thing you need to know about is NICAP."

NICAP, the National Investigations Committee on Aerial Phenomena, was the brainchild of a somewhat maverick physicist named Thomas Townsend Brown, and was established in 1956, the very same year that saw the publication of Gray Barker's *They Knew Too Much*

189

About Flying Saucers. For the most part, the members of the group were staunch advocates of the theory that UFOs have alien origins. NICAP was known for utilizing science and clear thinking with respect to UFO investigations, and was certainly the most well-respected public UFO research body in the United States from its beginnings to the mid-1960s. At least part of that respect was borne out of NICAP's prestigious board of governors, which included Vice Admiral Roscoe H. Hillenkoetter, who was the first head of the CIA, and Rear Admiral Delmer S. Fahrney, chief of the U.S. Navy's guided-missile project.

There are those, however, who believe that certain NICAP investigators significantly overstepped their bounds on a number of occasions when interviewing UFO witnesses. The result was that they may very well have come across as genuine Men in Black. Moseley, for example, is absolutely sure that just such a scenario occurred at the height of the NICAP days: "Doesn't a name like that—the National Investigations Committee on Aerial Phenomena—sound like an official government group, to you? They *weren't* official, of course; they were just UFO researchers, like me and you, really. But, if you're some yokel out in the sticks who has seen a UFO, and maybe it gets mentioned in the press, and someone comes to your door and flashes a NICAP ID card and says 'I don't want you to talk about this,' you might think it's the government, or those Men in Black that people talk about. And some of the NICAP people *would* say that because what every saucer group wants is the exclusive on the story."

Jim Moseley's perspective is echoed by Brad Steiger: "I'm quite certain that in some cases—and I actually accused some of the officials of this organization face-to-face—NICAP were responsible for some of the Men in Black tales. I *know* that some of their pimple-faced teenagers were coming up to people's houses, ringing doorbells, and saying: 'I'm from NICAP, the National Investigations Committee on Aerial Phenomena from Washington, D.C.'" Steiger continues, "You wouldn't have to push it too far when people heard the words 'from Washington' and the person flashes a little identity card, to think you have been visited by the Men in Black. And there's no field of paranormal research that is more jealous than the UFO field. So, if these pimpled teenagers are thinking, 'This is my case; this one belongs to me,' then they might have taken—or confiscated—photos and evidence from the witnesses and warned people, 'Don't talk to anyone else.' So, I think that definitely accounted for some of the Men in Black stories."

The scenario of researchers being perceived as Men in Black occurs across the pond as well. Back in 1958 an author named Gavin Gibbons penned a science-fiction novel titled *By Space Ship to the Moon*, the subject of which was the landing of an alien spacecraft on the Berwyn Mountain Range in North Wales, Great Britain. Some might say that Gibbons was a true prophet: On the night of January 23, 1974, an event occurred in the Berwyns that has come to be known within the UFO research community as the British Roswell. It confounded the locals and provoked a cascade of rumors and stories to the effect that an alien spacecraft had crashed on the mountains. Further rumors suggested that a secret military operation was put into place to recover the UFOs and its unearthly crew, and then transfer the remains to secure governmental establishments for study. Since that fateful night, the issue of what did or did not occur in the Berwyn Mountains has been the subject of several books, intense controversy, heated debate, and, at times, fury. That *something* happened at around 8:30 p.m. on the night in question is not in doubt, however.

Tales of strange lights in the sky, explosions in the Berwyns, cordoned-off mountain roads, and government conspiracies to hide the dark, alien truth abound, and have done so for decades. Researcher Andy Roberts, however, takes a more down-to-earth approach to the story. He believes that the UFO-crash scenario was nothing more than the misperception of a meteorite shower and a localized earth tremor, poachers at work on the dark mountainside armed with powerful lamps, and paranoia and rumor run rampant. Others believe that a military aircraft carrying Top Secret equipment crashed on the Berwyn range. But whatever the truth of that strange January 1974 affair, it also gave rise to an MIB legend.

During the course of his intense research into the case, Roberts learned that, at the height of the controversy, sensational rumors were flying around at a local level. They were rumors—spread in hushed tones—of mysterious officials descending on the scene to investigate the curious series of events. One person, Val Walls, told Roberts, "There were people staying at the local pub who didn't bother with anybody. There were two guys staying there but they never came into the pub. They slept there. They didn't communicate with anybody; they definitely kept themselves to themselves" (Roberts 2010).

A further story comes from Jenny Randles, a long-time researcher and author of the UFO phenomenon who resides in the British Isles. In January 1997, when, somewhat ironically, she had just completed writing her own book on the Men in Black, Randles paid a visit to her bank in the town of Buxton, where she was living at the time. As she left the bank, Randles was startled by the sight of an old, dark Jaguar displaying a 1962 license plate. A smartly dressed man in a suit stood by the vehicle, and had his eyes firmly fixed on the astonished UFO author. That Randles had personally investigated a number of British MIB cases in which the mystery men were driving black Jaguars only increased the tension.

Was Randles about to be silenced by a British-based Man in Black? Not at all. She elected to approach the man, and learned that he was simply a devotee of vintage cars.

Just occasionally, as this chapter has demonstrated, a Man in Black is merely an innocent party who happens to be dressed in dark clothes.

18

G-Men

In rare instances we can definitively prove that the secret hand of officialdom was at work. I am talking, of
course, about those cases in which the Men in Black
originated not from outer space, the depths of the human
mind, some unfathomable netherworld, or as a result of
mistaken identity, but from within the bowels of government itself. Granted, such 100-percent verifiable cases are
very few and far between, but they most assuredly *do*
exist—although most of them seem to date from decades
past, rather than from the modern era.

In 1968, British UFO researcher John Harney wrote
an article on the Men in Black that referenced a UFO case
that contained more than a few MIB elements. Harney
said that in February 1960, a man named Joe Perry, a
resident of Grand Blanc, Michigan, took a photograph of
an alleged UFO, and was soon thereafter visited by two
mysterious, dark-suited men posing as FBI agents who
duly confiscated his presumed otherworldly evidence.

The words of Harney strongly suggest that if Perry's visitors were *posing* as agents of the FBI, then they clearly had to have had very different origins, correct? Wrong. The Freedom of Information Act has allowed us to dig further into the Perry saga, and doing so has demonstrated that Perry's Men in Black really *were* FBI agents!

Now-declassified FBI files tell an intriguing story: Perry, who at the time of his UFO experience operated a pizza restaurant in Grand Blanc, Michigan, had, recorded the FBI, "been a professional photographer for 30 years," and often took pictures of the moon with his homemade telescope. At around 1 a.m. on February 21, 1960, Perry told two visiting FBI agents, after his story was published in the pages of the local *Flint Journal* newspaper, that on the night at issue he took a number of photographs of the moon, duly developed them in his very own darkroom, and while looking at them later, was astonished to notice that one showed what appeared to be nothing less than "a flying object somewhere between the end of his telescope and the surface of the moon" (Federal Bureau of Investigation 1960).

A highly excited Perry quickly had the picture blown up, which made the unidentified object much clearer. As he carefully scrutinized the new version of the photograph, he could see that it appeared to show a clearly delineated, structured vehicle that was oval-shaped, had a flat bottom, seemed to be surrounded by a fluorescent glow, and even appeared to have "a vapor trail running behind it." The FBI agents noted in their report that Perry "has taken over one thousand pictures of the moon and has never seen anything resembling this object" (Federal Bureau of Investigation 1960).

Certain that he had captured something truly anomalous on film, Perry duly furnished the two FBI agents with the original, priceless photograph, and they then sent it to the Office of Special Investigations at Selfridge Air Force Base. The photo was never seen again—at least, not outside of official channels. Notably, when this particularly conspiratorial aspect of the story reached the media, the *Flint Journal* chose to quote the words of a spokesperson for the National Investigations Committee on Aerial Phenomena (NICAP), who had informed Perry, much to his justified concern as it later transpired, that, "From past experience with photographic evidence we consider it unlikely that you will ever see your picture again" (Wilhelm 1960).

An angry Perry responded by contacting the FBI, which merely commented that the picture was now in the "proper hands," to which Perry responded, "The only way I will be satisfied if I don't get it back is if the government tells me it is top secret" (Wilhelm 1960). In the weeks and months that followed, a considerable file was built up by the FBI with respect to Perry's photograph, much of which dealt with his concerns about trying to retrieve his personal property from officialdom.

Matters were resolved, to the satisfaction of the FBI and the Air Force Office of Special Investigations at least, when, according to the official documentation on the affair, Perry was duly advised that "what appeared to be a flying object in this slide is actually a part of the negative which was not properly developed." Naturally, this statement did very little to satisfy those who insisted that the photograph genuinely showed some form of structured vehicle that had its origins on another world—and particularly so Joseph Perry, who viewed the whole situation through mystified and suspicious eyes (Wilhelm 1960).

Possibly recognizing that this controversy was only going to continue unless quick steps were taken to curb the situation, the FBI insisted to all inquirers that this was a matter for the Air Force, and only the Air Force, and thus duly steered all incoming letters in their direction. In time, the controversy surrounding the matter of Joseph Perry's missing photograph faded away—but not before, as a formerly classified FBI document reveals, FBI Director J. Edgar Hoover ominously wrote with respect to the involvement of the *Flint Journal* in promoting Joseph Perry's story: "It was necessary for this Bureau to straighten the record with that newspaper" (Federal Bureau of Investigation 1960).

This story contains all of the central facets of countless Men in Black incidents: There was Perry's initial photograph of a UFO that kicked off the controversy; then there is the fact that the same photograph subsequently vanished into oblivion after being handed over to two characters flashing government identity cards who, given that they were FBI agents, were likely dressed in dark suits and Fedora- or Homburg-style hats; and there was the veiled allusion to the possibility that the local media may even have been intimidated into silence about the case. If today we did not have open access to the FBI's files on Joseph Perry's 1960 UFO experience, this case might justifiably be placed within a Men in Black context. That we *do* have the files, however, is evidence that at least *some* MIB do indeed originate within the world of officialdom.

Acclaimed UFO expert Brad Steiger has said, "There were *definitely* people—military, FBI, or whoever—who did come around in the early years of flying saucers to check things out, because I had a journalist friend who thought all of this—UFOs—was nonsense."

Steiger's friend soon learned that UFOs were certainly not nonsense. One night, while in his office, Steiger heard what sounded very much like someone creeping up the outside stairs. He was not wrong: Upon opening the door, Steiger saw it was his friend. "He was a tough guy," recalls Steiger, "but that night he was on the verge of tears. He had spotted what he thought was a UFO—in his mind, 'those crazy things that Brad was talking about all the time'—and he had taken some pictures. And earlier that night, at his hotel room, there were three men, which he swears were Air Force officers. And they told him he must deliver the film and hand everything over. Of course, as a journalist who earns his living with a camera, he refused. Finally, they got rough and they said, 'This is for your good and the good of your country, the good of your world and the good of the universe.' It was straight out of the Men in Black. So, his question to me was along the lines of, 'Is all this stuff real?' He *did* surrender the film."

And as Steiger admits, "Some military people may not have polished up on their manners and did come across as a little brusque."

For yet another example that proves some Men in Black *are* government operatives, we have to leap forward two years after the Joseph Perry affair. We also have to make a quick trip across the pond.

Between 1991 and 1994, Nick Pope, a now-retired employee of the British Ministry of Defense who was attached to an outfit of the MoD called the Secretariat of the Air Staff, spent approximately 20 percent of his working week officially investigating UFO sightings and encounters, specifically from within the confines of his office. In other words, Pope never conducted on-site investigations of UFO activity, nor did he ever visit the homes of UFO witnesses to conduct personal, face-to-face interviews. Although a firm believer in the notion that some UFOs have extraterrestrial origins, he takes a very dim view of the idea that some Men in Black might be clandestinely operating from within certain British government and military departments and traveling the country silencing witnesses.

Pope solidly related his opinions to me on such matters:

> Men in Black stories? From what I understand, at some of these UFO conferences, the front rows are taken up by Walter Mitty–type characters who dress in black with sunglasses and take notes on everything. If there was one thing that anyone who was trying to be unobtrusive would not do, it would be that. I think any allegations about people turning up on someone's doorstep

and wanting to know about UFO sightings, what you're dealing with is either people who are lying, and saying it happened when it didn't, or, perhaps more likely, people who have genuinely been visited by someone, but where that someone is some Walter Mitty–type character who likes to think he's some sort of James Bond secret agent. If anyone's going around saying "You must keep quiet about that," it's the exact opposite of what we do at the Ministry of Defense. So, it's nothing to do with us.

As earnest as Nick Pope's words are, they are way off target, as the British Freedom of Information Act has now acutely demonstrated. Pope never left the confines of the MoD to investigate even a single a UFO case, but others, attached to different official departments with their own secret agendas, most certainly did. On the night of August 30, 1962, a teenage girl named Anne Henson had her life turned upside down when both a UFO and a Man in Black entered her otherwise normal life.

At the time, Henson was 16, still at school, and living on a dairy farm in the county of Somerset with her parents. One day she woke up—or, perhaps, was woken up—during the early hours of the morning. She sat up in bed and could see through the window what looked like a round ball of light in the sky. It appeared to change color from red to green to yellow, and seemed to contain at its center "a circle with rays of light coming from it....

At first I thought it was a star, but it wasn't static. Then I thought that it must be a helicopter or something like that, but there was absolutely no sound from it. Well, it then began moving backwards and forwards and went from left to right. I was very intrigued by it because it was making fairly rapid movements. But it was the colors of the lights that attracted me first; they were nice bright colors. It would come towards me quite quickly and appeared to increase in size, and then reversed and moved sideways at a middle speed. But it always returned to its original position just above the hills.

Over an hour or so, the light gradually receded until it was just like a pinprick of light. Well, I went to sleep, but the next night I wondered if it might be there again—and it was. This happened on a few occasions, and I got quite used to seeing it when it was a clear night. To be honest, I got quite friendly with it, really. I didn't feel threatened by it, because although it came close to our farm, it didn't come *that* close. Now, when I'd seen it a few times, I decided that I would get a compass and graph paper and try to track where it was coming from because this was intriguing me. I thought: this is a bit different.

Understandably unsure of what the mysterious object was, Henson decided to write a letter to a nearby Royal Air Force base to see if they might be able to shed some meaningful light on her mystifying late-night encounters: "After I saw the light for a few times and tracked the movements of it, I contacted [Royal Air Force base] Chivenor. I told them what I'd seen and then I got a letter saying that my sighting was being looked at. Then this chap turned up at the house."

That's right, a Man in Black was about to put in an appearance: "It was an evening when he arrived for the first time, and he pulled up in this old black car, and when he came in the house he was wearing a black suit and tie. I would imagine that he was in his late 30s, and I was most disappointed that he wasn't wearing a uniform. He announced himself as a Royal Air Force official, and, of course, I took it as such. To me, he was an authority, put it like that. He actually came to visit me on several occasions. I *assumed* he was from RAF Chivenor; he didn't actually say so. I was a bit overawed that somebody was actually coming to see me."

"Altogether," Henson says of her dark-suited visitor, "he came on three nights. On the first night he came up to my bedroom and we sat there waiting for the clouds to clear. Unfortunately, that night and the next night he came, we couldn't see anything. So, he said that he would have to come back again. Now, on the third night, he saw it." Henson's Man in Black was not about to reveal to Henson his own thoughts on the nature of the aerial phenomenon, however: "He was very cagey. He wasn't very friendly, but he wasn't nasty either. But on this night he took some photos of the light. He didn't seem very surprised by what he saw. It was all very, very low-key, which I suppose is the way to play it if it was something unusual. If he'd have got excited, I'd have got excited. He then left and he took his camera and took my compass drawings and notes—and I never got them back. But before going he said that nobody else would believe what I'd seen and there was no point in me talking about it at school. At that age, you don't want to be laughed at—and my family had laughed at me anyway."

Henson's account, though containing all the elements of a classic MIB visitation, differs in one striking aspect: The official files on her experience have now been declassified by the British government, and they identify her mysterious visitor as Sergeant J.W. Scott, at the time an employee of the British Royal Air Force's elite Provost and Security Services—the equivalent of the United States's Air Force Office of Special Investigations (AFOSI), and whose work revolves around espionage, counterespionage, and disinformation- and deception-based programs that have a bearing upon national security and the defense of the realm. Here, then, is yet another example of a story that may very well have forever languished in anomalous Men in Black territory, had it not been for the fact that the files on Henson's experience were, decades later, quietly declassified into the public domain by the British Ministry of Defense.

UFO researcher and author William L. Moore has uncovered evidence further suggesting that at least *some* MIB are nothing more than the tools of officialdom. His research has suggested that such individuals are, in reality, government people in disguise, who originate with a unit of U.S. Air Force Intelligence known currently as the Air Force Special Activities Center (AFSAC). Moore's research suggested that the history of the AFSAC can be traced back to the 1127th Field Activities Group—an oddball unit whose job was to get people to talk. Recruited into the group, Moore elaborated, were just the type of people that might make perfect Men in Black: safe-crackers, cat burglars, lock-pickers, impersonators, assorted masters of deception, and useful flakes of numerous types.

Researcher Chris O'Brien has an interesting take on this angle: "I think the more mundane element—that's the intelligence guys, the military guys—knows about the high-strangeness element: the *real* Men in Black. And they play with that: wearing the wigs and make-up and taking the lead from the weirder stories to cover their tracks. So, there are probably at least two things going on: there's the definite high-strangeness Men in Black, and then there's the people in the intelligence community using that same image to their own advantage."

Allen Greenfield shares this conclusion: "I've entertained the notion that whatever governmental agency might have been trying to frighten UFO witnesses and UFO organizations may have been imitating whatever this paranormal phenomena is; and that's what I regard it as: paranormal phenomena. My general feeling is that some of the cases that are lumped in with the Men in Black probably are governmental investigations of cases, and maybe even government efforts to confuse the issue of who the Men in Black are."

It's also worth noting Greg Bishop's words on this facet of the MIB controversy: "The intelligence guys really might have worn the makeup and wigs that the witnesses report, just to spook them out, and to help confiscate any evidence the person has; it covers their tracks. That seems more likely, to me, than strange beings running around with wigs and makeup. But, it admittedly doesn't explain *all* the cases, so maybe it's not just a mythos that was created by the intelligence community. Maybe the intelligence people just *expanded* on real stories, and maybe there really *are* MIB out there, *other* MIB, *real* MIB—the weirder ones, I mean."

And speaking of those weirder Men in Black, it's high time for us to revisit them once again.

Time Travelers

Certainly one of the most controversial theories on the true nature of the Men in Black is that, rather than space-faring entities, government agents, Tricksters, or Tulpas, they are actually time travelers from our own distant future!

Is our present day *really* playing host to clandestine time-surfers from a future that is as far ahead of us as it is incomprehensible? Or is such a scenario just too fantastic and absurd for words? Maybe not: John Keel came across numerous cases that focused upon the unknown visitors' odd obsession with time. Indeed, he noted that their often-reported ultra-fast mode of conversation "could be caused by their failure to adjust to our time cycle when they enter our space-time continuum. They are talking at a faster rate because their time is different from ours" (Keel 1975).

And of course there is the curious fact that in count-less reports on record, the Men in Black are seen driving

209

old-style cars that seem to be incomprehensibly brand-new. And what of those homburg and fedora hats with which the Men in Black seem so enamored? They were certainly all the rage in the 1940s and 1950s, but they are most definitely less so now. Indeed, practically everything about the MIB seems strangely out of time. If the time-travel scenario does have some validity, then perhaps these anomalies are due to the Men in Black occasionally slipping up when trying to gauge the fashions and modes of transport of the many eras to which they are constantly traveling.

Beyond the Men in Black, some researchers and witnesses to UFO activity believe that the pilots of the elusive saucer-shaped craft themselves may not be extraterrestrials, but instead time travelers from our own distant future. Dr. Bruce Goldberg, who holds a BA degree in biology and chemistry, and who has penned more than 20 books, including *Past Lives, Future Lives*, is an adherent of this particular theory. He says that the entities piloting the UFOs "...originate from between 1,000 to 3,000 years in our future and from earth.... These time travelers have mastered the art of entering the fifth dimension and traveling back in time to our century.... The purpose... is to facilitate our spiritual growth. They are us in the future" (Goldberg 2010).

Jim Penniston, formerly of the U.S. Air Force, also believes UFOs are piloted by future humans. He was one of the key military players in a famous UFO encounter at Rendlesham Forest, Suffolk, England—an atmospheric, densely treed area adjacent to the now-closed joint British Royal Air Force/U.S. Air Force military complex of Bentwaters-Woodbridge—on December 26 and 28, 1980. Essentially, what many UFO researchers believe took place deep in the dark woods throughout the course of several nights was the landing of a craft—or, perhaps, multiple crafts—from another world, from which small, humanoid entities reportedly emerged and engaged senior U.S. military personnel in face-to-face communication. The craft was allegedly tracked on radar, deposited elevated traces of radiation within the depths of the forest, avoided capture, and made good its escape—and in so doing created a controversy that rages to this day.

Penniston underwent hypnotic regression in 1994 as part of an attempt to recall deeply buried data relative to what occurred during one of Britain's closest encounters. While under hypnosis, Penniston stated that our presumed aliens are, in reality, visitors from a far-flung future. That future, Penniston added, is very dark, and in deep trouble: polluted, deathly cold, and blighted by reproductive problems. The answer to their problems is to travel into the distant past—to our present day, in other words—to secure sperm, eggs, and chromosomes, all as part of an effort to ensure the continuation of the dwindling human race.

The skeptics ask, "Where is the hard evidence to support such a scenario?" And, on the matter of the revelations of Jim Penniston, the skeptic may suggest that data secured from someone placed into a radically altered state of mind may not be entirely reliable, even if the character of the person relating the story is unblemished. In other words, hypnosis may be just as likely to bring forth fantasies borne out of the murky depths of the subconscious and the imagination as it is to produce real data.

But what does any of this have to do with the Men in Black? A fascinating theory has been put forward that portrays the MIB as time travelers from a future that is millennia ahead of our present. It is the theory of Joshua P. Warren, one of the world's premier investigative researchers and authors on all things supernatural and mysterious. Warren's theory begins with one important question: "Why do they wear black?" While deeply pondering this important point, Warren developed a hypothesis that "combines the very complex with the very mundane," and that provides us with a potential explanation as to who the MIB really may be.

Joshua P. Warren in his paranomal HQ.

"I have thought, for a long time, about what I call the para-temporal loop hypothesis. At first glance it may not seem all that original, as it deals with the complexities that derive from potential time travel. The hypothesis is based upon one particular testable element. And that is, if ever, in all of the infinite future, any advanced species discovers how to travel back in time, will they do it?" Warren notes that if time travel is truly impossible to achieve, then the hypothesis crumbles and it becomes something to simply muse upon instead. But, he stresses, if it is indeed feasible to travel into the past, and then back to the future again, then not only *will* someone, someday, attempt it, but they will very likely keep such a fantastic discovery cloaked in secrecy, too. "It's just about the most powerful secret anyone could have: the ability to change the course of time," he says.

Here is how Warren sees the mind-bending scenario playing out:

> Let's say, hypothetically, that one million years from now—long after humans are gone, perhaps—there is a humanoid creature that dominates this planet that has evolved from the oceans. We'll call him Fish-Man. And Fish-Man is a great scientist and has discovered how to travel back in time. And so he does this. And let's say he goes back to the year 1920. Of course, he has to do his best to disguise his appearance, or else everyone will know what he is. And while he's back in 1920, he might be thinking how he could help, or even hurt, his own future existence. And in doing so, he wants to be careful that he *doesn't* harm himself in the future. On the contrary, he might even try and enhance his future life by changing something in the past that will benefit him down the road; or even something that will harm his enemies.

Such an action would not be without its hazards, however, as Warren readily admits:

> Now, of course, Fish-Man will never know for certain if it's going to turn out right. If he screws up, then maybe he starts to vanish like the kid in *Back to the Future*. But if he does a good job, then he returns to his future and he finds that he has a better life. But, by traveling back in time, he has caused a para-temporal loop. It's a separate timeline that he continues to exist on. So, continuing with this thought experiment, let's say he gets back to his future, and things are better and brighter for him. And he doesn't want to jeopardize that by stating what he has done. But, he wakes up one day and everything is back the way it was before he tweaked it by going into the past. And he can't figure out what's happened.

Unbeknownst to Fish-Man, about a billion years after he's alive, Bear-Man becomes the next scientist who figures how to travel in time, long after the Fish-People are gone. Bear-Man is a humanoid who has evolved from the forests. He travels back to 1915, and makes a number of changes from which he will profit, but that will affect, or even completely cancel out, the timeline carefully altered and nurtured by Fish-Man. And, at that complicated point, all hell inevitably breaks loose, as Warren details:

> Fish-Man has to then go back to 1910 to correct Bear-Man's adjustments, and so on, and so on. So, now, we have what seems like the plot of some bad sci-fi movie, where we have all these figures from different futures that are going

back into the past and trying to tweak things to their own benefit. But, if you look at this in a broader scale, and consider that the future apparently has some infinity about it, then there may be thousands and thousands of these different types of beings that are each traveling back, tweaking the timelines in some way. And what makes it an even bigger mess is that they're not necessarily aware of each other. They're all just as confused about what's happening as everybody else is.

As first-class evidence of such chaotic meddling with the timelines, Warren refers to the strange story of what has become known as the Thunderbird Photograph. As the tale goes, back in the 1960s, a photograph, said to date from the late 1800s, appeared in the pages of a newsstand magazine of the day—possibly *True*, *Saga*, or *Argosy*—displaying the deceased remains of a monstrous bird pinned to a pair of barn doors somewhere in rural North America (the exact location is, just like the picture itself, a matter of some debate). Numerous researchers, investigators, and authors of a whole range of anomalies claim that they personally saw the priceless picture when it was published. The big problem today, however, is that, despite the fact that the pages of the three magazines (and many others besides) have been carefully and dutifully scoured—even to the point of obsession—the picture cannot be found anywhere. It's almost as if it never existed in the first place. And, in a curious way, maybe it didn't. Or, if Joshua P. Warren's theories are correct, maybe it did exist—but only for a short while.

How can we explain such a strange situation? A specific photograph cannot simply disappear from *every* publication that it ever appeared in—can it? Maybe, if we follow Warren's lead, it can: "I get the impression," he says, "that there might be a shifting timeline that we are passing through on a day-by-day basis. One day UFOs might be real, and the next they're not. The next day Bigfoot is running around your backyard, and the next day he doesn't exist. One day the Thunderbird photo is in a magazine, and then when the timeline is played with again, it's no longer in the magazine. And it may be that, day by day, hour by hour, or even minute by minute, small changes to the timeline are being made by these entities, or beings, coming back and constantly playing around with the past and the future. So, things we remember in the past, like the Thunderbird photo, suddenly no longer exist in the present."

And it's with respect to this particular aspect of time travel, Warren opines, that the Men in Black may play some form of critical role: "If we accept it might be possible that something similar to what I've just described might be happening, or potentially happening, then somewhere along the line we can imagine that there might be policemen—time-cops, so to speak—who step in here and there, and who try to really get the scoop on all these para-temporal loops and control the entire situation."

And that, Warren suggests, brings us to the presence and role of the Men in Black: "Going back to my original point: Why do the MIB dress like this? Why do we call them the Men in Black? Well, if a man puts on a black suit with a black hat and walks down the street in 1910, and you see that man, you would probably notice him. But, would you think there was anything too extraordinary, or too out-of-place about him? No, you probably would not. And if you saw a man walking down the street in 2010 wearing a black suit and a black hat, would you notice him? Probably, yes. But, would you think you think there was necessarily anything too extraordinary? No."

What this all demonstrates, says Warren, is that the outfit of the black suit and the black hat is flexible enough to work within the social context of the culture of at least a century or more. And so, therefore, if you are someone who is in the time-travel business, and within the course of your workday you're going to go to 1910 to take care of some business, and then a couple of hours later you're going to be in 1985, and then a few hours after that you'll be heading to 2003, you don't want to be in a position of having to change your clothes three times. So what do you do? In Warren's hypothesis, you dress in an outfit that is going to allow you access to the longest period of time within which that same outfit may not draw too much unwelcome attention. "And that's why," suggests Warren "in and around the whole 20th century, it just so happens that the black suit and the black hat will work for them."

What if, however, your time-travel plans are destined to take you much farther into the past? Clearly, wearing a 20th-century suit just won't cut it. Warren acknowledges this point when he says, "If you were to go back into the 1600s or 1700s, there would be a different wardrobe that would work within the broadest range. I don't know what that wardrobe is, but I feel confident that if I sat down with a historian who was extremely knowledgeable of the fashions from those past periods, and who also understood the concept that I'm talking about, we could probably come up with a dress that the Men in Black may have worn at various points throughout history, in order to give them the widest range to work within at any given time."

Perhaps those earlier Men in Black, those time travelers who chose to head even further into our past, may have been the prosperous and mysterious burghers in black to which Brad Steiger referred in a previous chapter.

Warren also weaves one of the most notorious fringe elements of the Men in Black puzzle into his paradigm-mangling ideas, too: that of Mothman. Could it really be the case that the shadowy, glowing-eyed beast that briefly haunted Point Pleasant's long-abandoned TNT area in the mid-1960s was a real-life equivalent of Warren's hypothetical Bear-Man or Fish-Man? And, if so, were Point Pleasant's Men in Black dispatched from a faraway future to bring the activities of this winged nightmare to a halt? Warren thinks this may be *exactly* what occurred:

> When it comes to the idea of Mothman, this brings up another good connection to what I was describing. If you have a situation in which the timelines are being constantly changed in an unauthorized way, by some of these para-temporal travelers, from far in the future, who are unleashing all this bizarre stuff that isn't supposed to be there—and maybe a real Mothman, like the hypothetical Bear-Man and Fish-Man, is actually one of these para-temporal travelers—then obviously you're going to have these Men in Black pop up there to try to get the timeline

situation under control. And that's why, when you take something like what happened at Point Pleasant in the 1960s, we have a variety, a whole spectrum of paranormal activity and strange creatures, and then the Men in Black suddenly appear.

So, it could be that the Men in Black follow all this stuff around; that's their job. Not that they are causing these things to happen, but they're alerted to it when there's a dangerous timeline issue that needs to be corrected. They're not necessarily the bad guys at all; they might be doing damage control, and maybe that includes warning and silencing witnesses to protect the time-travel secret. They might be weird, and they might look weird, but their overall mission may be just to keep order and protect the timelines.

How ironic it would be if the theories of Joshua P. Warren are indeed correct, and that instead of representing our absolute worst nightmare—as many that have encountered the MIB surely believe them to be—the Men in Black are actually heroes: the dutiful, persistent guardians of past, present, and future combined, forever fated to keeping their strange secrets from those who cross their paths as they surf the centuries, always on missions to terminate endless numbers of meddlesome, reckless time manipulators.

Demons and the Occult

Ray Boeche is an Anglican priest who served as the rector of the Celebration Anglican Church in Lincoln, Nebraska, for nearly a decade. He is also the founder and the former director of the Fortean Research Center, a former Nebraska state director for the worldwide Mutual UFO Network, and the recipient of a BA from Peru State College and a Master of Theology degree from St. Mark's School of Divinity. As someone with insight into both Christianity and the UFO controversy, and who has studied the many complexities of the MIB mystery extensively, Boeche opines today that, "Ultimately, I think a demonic deception is the foundation from which the Men in Black phenomenon springs." This belief closely matches the conclusion of Claudia Cunningham, whose Man in Black experience was detailed earlier in this book.

The idea that the UFO presence in our world may have demonic origins is not a new one. The theory has been

Ray Boeche is an Anglican priest who has deeply studied the MIB phenomenon.

carefully addressed in a number of books, including *UFO End-Time Delusion*, written by David Allen Lewis and Robert Shreckhise; my own *Final Events*; and John Weldon and Zola Levitt's *UFOs: What on Earth Is Happening?* Perhaps more than anyone else, however—and chiefly as a direct result of his combined background within the Christian Church and with the Mutual UFO Network—Boeche should be seen as someone in a prime position to comment on this particular theory. That Boeche—as we will now see—was also personally acquainted, to varying degrees, with both Albert Bender and Gray Barker makes his conclusions relative to the MIB conundrum all the more important. "I was actually in touch with Albert Bender in the early to mid-'70's," Boeche says, "which was years after his Men in Black experience. This was in California, when he was involved in helping preserve the work of film composer Max Steiner, and he just would not discuss it: the experience, the Men in Black, none of it. It had obviously affected him."

Boeche had much more success when it came to Barker: "I was a kid when I was first in contact with Barker, and stayed in contact right up until a few months before he passed away. He was always helpful on the phone and in correspondence; he was a very amenable guy. From the contact and conversations I had with Barker, I do think something happened with Bender. Just how much of the actual written account we have is confabulation and how much is exaggeration, I don't know. But something did happen to Bender, and it may very well have involved FBI agents. And I tend to think that Bender's experience was precipitated by a visit from someone in the government."

Boeche explains his views on this integral aspect of the Bender affair:

> Bender may well have been visited by FBI agents. And that whole image of black suits and threats that were possibly playing on Bender's mind may have dictated how these forces, Bender's MIB, appeared for him as his involvement with the occult proceeded and he had the experience in his bedroom. He did have a longstanding fascination with the occult, and I think that the FBI visit could have had a definite impact on how he might have experienced these other things, and how "they" might have appeared to him in a context that would serve their ends: the dark suits and hats. There's a distinct possibility that the phenomenon was pulling this imagery—the FBI agents, black suits, and their visit and warnings—out of Bender's subconscious and masquerading as something connected to the saucer people to lure him further into the occult.

Boeche continues: "There's a lot we can take from some of the early research into psychedelics, where the major thrust of what type of experience the person would have would be dictated by mindset and setting. And I think that ties into the Bender story, in a sense. I think there's this idea that if we open ourselves to outside influences—I'm speaking in spiritual terms here—or we seek contact or an experience with an alien, then you assume it to be that—an alien—if and when it appears." However, "It may not be what it purports to be. I think these forces can play on our own mental predispositions of what we expect to see."

Boeche notes what he sees as the hazards that may manifest when one takes the proverbial plunge into the darkest of all waters and engages such black-hearted entities, as Bender most certainly did:

> I have always thought that one of the most important things that John Keel ever said was that if you have kids or teenagers, this is not something to encourage them to get involved with. Keel was a pretty dyed-in-the-wool atheist. But he understood that, at some level, there's something in some sense transcendent over us, that can, if nothing else, "mess" with us. And it can cause a lot of damage.... Sometimes, I think I'm singing a one-note song with this, from a Christian perspective. I would not consider myself theologically liberal or a theological fundamentalist. My beliefs are solidly orthodox, and rooted in my view of the Bible as God's inerrant Word. But there are things that we just aren't equipped to deal with

from a mechanistic, naturalistic worldview. There are malevolent forces out there that will be happy to take advantage of just about any opening we give them. And, so, we need to be very cautious. I tend to think that may be what happened to Albert Bender, but he might not have been so cautious.

In Boeche's view, Bender, already scared out of his wits by an intimidating visit from *real* FBI agents, was then further tormented by paranormal entities that invaded his subconscious, coldly hauled the FBI-style Man in Black imagery from the depths of his mind, and adopted nearly identical guises to achieve their aims of assaulting, deceiving, and manipulating poor Bender.

Moving on from the Bender experience, Boeche notes that Reginald Scot—in *The Discoverie of Witchcraft*, published in 1584—described the Devil as being repugnant in appearance. Similarly, Charles Wall, in his 1902 book, *Devils*, cited an 11th-century Greek manuscript in which the Devil appears humanlike. Traditionally, the Devil must also possess some perceivable defect when appearing in human form, very much like the Men in Black who walk awkwardly or display some other obvious physical defect.

In addition, Boeche identifies connections between the Men in Black and the Eastern mystical tradition's enigmatic Brothers of the Shadow, whom Michael Talbot calls "cunning and evil; intent upon keeping the student of the occult from finding out the proverbial answer. The Brothers of the Shadow, like the MIB, are known

for threatening students whenever they get too close"
(Boeche lecture 1994).

Also on the historical angle, Boeche demonstrates
that the Men in Black, in the early 1900s, were seemingly skulking around the bleak, dark hills and valleys
of Wales, Great Britain, at the *very same time* that a variety of unidentified aerial phenomena was also putting
in an unwelcome appearance. Specifically, Boeche drew
my attention to a 1905 article that appeared within the
pages of the *Barmouth Advertiser* newspaper and that
reads, "In the neighborhood dwells an exceptionally
intelligent young woman of the peasant stock, whose
bedroom has been visited three nights in succession by
a man dressed in black. This figure has delivered a message to the girl which she is too frightened to relate"
(*Barmouth Advertiser* 1905). That this particular encounter occurred when the good folk of Wales were also
experiencing sightings of mysterious, unidentified aerial
lights provides much food for thought. Furthermore,
Boeche points out, "It is interesting to note that this
event comes in the midst of the great Welsh Christian
revival of 1904–05" (Boeche 1994).

By far one of the most important (and certainly most
disturbing) cases that Boeche believes offers direct support for the notion that the Men in Black have demonic
origins began in the late 1960s. It is a nightmarish tale of
malevolence, hostility, and unrelenting negativity—those
central themes on which the Men in Black seem to thrive.
It was after the man in question—whom Boeche describes as
"a researcher whose name would be recognized by everyone
involved in UFO research"—had been deeply immersed in

the investigation of a number of UFO encounters that included low-level sightings of UFOs and one case involving UFO occupants that he started to receive a series of alarming and harassing telephone calls.

"Many times there would be nothing on the line," Boeche explains. "Often a strange, metallic whistling sound, mixed with what he could only describe as 'electronic noise' would be present. Sometimes a garbled voice speaking in an unintelligible language would be heard. Sometimes threats against himself or his family would be made by a voice that sounded vaguely 'unhuman.' Changing his telephone number didn't seem to help. The telephone company could find no tap on his line, and was never able to locate the perpetrator of the calls."

Then there came the mail tampering, very similar to that described earlier by both Greg Bishop and Chris O'Brien: Letters were delivered opened and torn, some mail went astray or completely vanished, and important case evidence disappeared en route to its destination. Most unsettling of all, Boeche reveals that the man "received numerous threats through the mail and many documents that consisted of odd hieroglyphic-like symbols with no explanation." Things were then taken to a different level when the phenomenon began to maliciously target the man's home. Boeche says, "On three different occasions, the office located in his home was ransacked, files rifled, and in two instances, research material of significance to current cases disappeared. This was made even more mysterious by virtue of the fact that his home was protected by an elaborate electronic security system connected directly to the police department. The alarm system was never triggered."

Of course, all of this could quite conceivably be the handiwork of government spooks, spies, lock-pickers, and espionage agents. What happened next, however, is very difficult—if not impossible—to reconcile with such a down-to-earth theory: There was a sudden and terrifying outbreak of poltergeist-like activity in the man's home. Household objects flew across rooms; doors were thrown open and slammed shut under their own volition; foul, sulfur-like smells plagued the family; enigmatic shapes and shadowy, unspeakable things skirted around corners and, in a few instances, raced through well-lit rooms toward some hapless person who would scream at the top of his lungs, bracing himself for some sort of violent, physical onslaught that never came—not for a while, anyway. Given that poltergeist manifestations have been associated with the actions of predatory, manipulative demons, this suggests whatever was afoot had nothing to do with the actions of government personnel.

On six different occasions, Boeche reveals, the researcher's wife, in the presence of at least two other people (on one occasion, in the presence of six others), was attacked by an invisible entity. The woman was slapped, clawed, bitten, punched, and thrown across the room by something that was invisible yet possessed of enough substance to raise welts on her face, gouge her arms, and leave animal-like teeth marks on her back and legs. Four of these attacks were followed almost immediately by telephone calls warning the researcher to, in the words of the caller, *leave the flying saucers alone*.

Then, some might say inevitably, an unwelcome visitor in black of the type we have come to know well came slithering out of the darkness. The researcher, on three different occasions, was approached by a prototypical Man in Black, described as about 6 feet 6 inches (1.98 m) tall and cadaverous in appearance, who made threats against the researcher. He experienced one visit at his home, one at work, and one at a restaurant while waiting for his wife to return from the restroom. The man, who described his state at the time that this occurred as one of abject terror, truly believed he was losing his mind, and was afraid that his wife might even be killed. As a result, he put his UFO research firmly behind him for an extended period of time.

Out of his in-depth research, coupled with his religious background, Boeche has come to a conclusion: "It becomes apparent that all aspects of the UFO phenomenon have manifested throughout human history, albeit in somewhat different and varying guises. The same can be said of, if you will, the very 'dark side' of ufology: the menacing activities of the MIB. The UFO phenomena are definitely culturally reflective" (Boeche 1994). If one starts with ancient accounts of humanity's interaction with deities, dragons, and demons, Boeche notes, one will find almost exact parallels between those historically recorded manifestations and what is occurring today. There is no substantial difference in the phenomenon, only in the cultural references we use to define it. In other words, one man's alien is another man's ghostly black dog; one man's werewolf is another man's Djinn; and one man's... well, you get the picture.

Boeche cites the words of the late author/researcher Ivan Sanderson, whose influence on paranormal research still resonates nearly 40 years after his untimely passing.

Sanderson asked: Are the Men in Black extraterrestrials, the descendants of extraterrestrials, or even the agents of extraterrestrials? Or, he wondered, do we need to allow for a totally new category of intelligent beings that are interacting with us? Boeche answers that "we must acknowledge a different category of being. We must awaken to the realization that we are caught in a web of deception, and that the web is closing in on us. We are being watched, probed, and manipulated by forces from outside our known physical universe. We are not alone, and we may not like it much when we find out what sort of company we have" (Boeche 1994).

Colin Bennett, who had an encounter with a Man in Black in London in the early 1980s (as described in Chapter 10), shares Boeche's suspicion that the Men in Black have occult origins. He uses our old friend Albert Bender as an example: "...before [his] marriage, [Bender] was a rather typical back-bedroom young person of his time: His room was decorated with symbols of all kinds of occult weirdness, and it resembled a kind of metaphysical temple. He did not take notice of warnings of all classical occultists—Paracelsus, Levi, and Crowley—that mystical occultism is not to be taken lightly. History gives plenty of examples of forms which can be summoned up to tell all kinds of tales to gullible human beings, always anxious to have the secrets to life, the universe, and everything."

Expanding on this line of thinking, Bennett says, "The celebrated warnings from MIB and 'extraterrestrial' aliens are the direct equivalents to the Christian warnings about tampering with Christian mysteries too deeply lest one might meet the Devil or one of his minions. Christian thinkers also gave warning about the dangers of independent and somewhat cavalier occult interpretations of the Incarnation, Transfiguration, and the character of the Holy Ghost. The warnings here were not so much about dangers of finding secret knowledge, but the risk of annihilation, long before any portals of such supposed knowledge were reached."

In other words, Bennett believes that when one goes looking for paranormal entities, or goes so far as to attempt to invoke them, they very often do appear. But, as he also notes, both the nature of these myriad beings and the stories they relate need to be viewed and analyzed via careful, guarded filters. To do otherwise is to risk such creatures getting their paranormal claws into us to a potentially disastrous degree—which appears to be precisely what happened to Bender, unfortunately for him.

Timothy Green Beckley has a disturbing Man in Black account to relate that may also be in line with Ray Boeche's views. It is a case that appears to involve full-blown paranormal possession: "There was one case where I might have been threatened by a Man in Black," Beckley reveals. "There was a publication I wrote for in the 1970s called *Official UFO*. They published their address in the magazine, so they did get a few crank visitors to the offices. One of these was a gentleman who claimed he was being stalked by the Men in Black."

In time, Beckley met the man, and in the late 1970s and early 1980s, became the unwelcome recipient of a series of very threatening calls from him. Beckley decided to call the police, and the man was soon traced: It transpired he was a homeless person staying in Grand Central Station. Beckley adds that the man "must have called 50 times and left crazy, threatening messages that would go on and on. I spoke with his parents, who were in Florida, and they said that although he wasn't always like this, something came over him now and again." Beckley suggests:

> With cases like this guy where something came over him, and with the MIB, it's like a possession, where a paranormal force takes possession of the person and they then *become* the Man in Black, doing what the force wants them to do, but without their knowledge. Afterward, they might not even remember any of it. These people are living on the fringe of society; they are simple-minded people who can easily be controlled and influenced. Someone, say, who might be living in some rundown apartment, is taken over in a kind of trance, and then he becomes one of the Men in Black. He threatens someone, and then he goes back to his normal life after the possession ends, and he doesn't remember it. But while he is under the control of whatever is doing this, he's not quite right. And like a zombie, is the best way I can describe it.

Particularly relevant to Boeche's views of MIB being more occult than extraterrestrial is the usage of Ouija boards by people who have seen a Man in Black. In 1954, George Hunt Williamson, a man who claimed repeated contacts with extraterrestrials in the 1950s, published a book called *The Saucers Speak*, which focused upon his well-publicized attempts to contact extraterrestrials via short-wave radio and Ouija boards. (Actar of Mercury, Adu of Hatonn in Andromeda, Agfa Affa of Uranus, Ankar-22 of Jupiter, and Artok of Pluto were just some of the many purported extraterrestrials with whom Williamson claimed interaction, but which others might conclude were deceptive demons.) Then, in the latter part of the 1950s, Williamson changed his name, drafted a fictitious academic and familial background to accompany his new identity, and essentially disappeared. He died in 1986, largely forgotten by the UFO research community that had briefly welcomed him into the fold in the 1950s.

Albert Bender, without whom there would simply not be an MIB phenomenon as we have come to understand it, was also a dabbler with Ouija boards. As well, Mary Robertson, whose Man in Black was photographed in 1968 by Timothy Green Beckley and Jim Moseley, was a big fan of the boards. And Claudia Cunningham's friend Linda, who had a Man in Black encounter at the Albany Rural Cemetery in May 2009, was also "into the Ouija boards." Could it only be chance and coincidence that several people who were attracted to Ouija boards were subsequently targeted for visitation by the MIB?

Conclusion

A nd now, dear reader, our complex journey into the multifaceted twilight realm of the Men in Black is at its end. What a wild and unsettling journey it has been. We've seen that what, for many, has long been perceived as a phenomenon having its roots *solely* in the realm of hoaxing, mistaken identity, government espionage, secret agents, and visitors from the Pentagon, the FBI, and the Department of Homeland Security, is actually nothing of the sort.

Yes, in *some* cases we *are* dealing with certain characters who lurk in positions of power, and who wish to keep us in the dark about what is really known about the UFO conundrum at a governmental level. And, yes, there *have* been cases of mistaken identity and hoaxing. But for the most part, when it comes to the Men in Black we are dealing with phenomena that are far, far stranger and much more terrifying than any government agent come to silence witnesses.

235

As we have seen, there may very well be *several* points of origin for the Men in Black. Some MIB, such as those experienced by Albert Bender, may have been born out of nothing stranger than repeated misfiring of the man's brain, coupled with a fertile, overactive, alien-dominated imagination that spent far too much time cooped up alone in a creepy, cobwebbed attic. But out of the sheer potency of this MIB imagery a horrific birth was given to Tulpas of three shadowy men that quickly found they very much enjoyed their newfound freedom and existence, and have ever since embarked upon a reign of terror as a means to continue their precarious existence in our world.

Given the close links that the Men in Black appear to have with psychic possession of the individual, Ouija boards, and poltergeist activity, it seems safe to conclude that their link with the occult is also a valid area of research that may unlock the secrets to yet another aspect of the MIB phenomenon, or perhaps even to a *related* aspect that we have yet to fully comprehend. As well, if the unique theories of Joshua P. Warren are correct—that some of the Men in Black may originate from a point far in our very own future—such startling revelations provoke and even demand major revisions to our scientific beliefs and teachings. That the past, present, and future may not be cast in stone, that all three might be in constant, dizzying states of flux, and that the MIB could be intimately involved in secretly protecting and manipulating countless time lines on a nearly infinite basis, is almost as weird as the black-suited visitors themselves!

Before you go, remember my careful advice in the Introduction: If you *do* decide to pursue the MIB, and you one day receive that dreaded slow knocking on your front door, for your sake and that of everyone you hold dear to your heart, let it remain firmly locked and unopened. If you fail to heed that advice, at the very least take careful and respectful notice of the following cautionary words of Brad Steiger, for they are the words of one who knows of what he speaks:

"The Men in Black are real, and if you truly devote yourself to pursuing this, then one can become in great danger. We're up against something that none of us can fully comprehend."

Glossary

anomaly Something that is abnormal, unexpected, and difficult to classify or explain.

anthropomorphize To attribute human form or behavior to things that are not human.

counterespionage Activity designed to detect and stop enemy spying.

cryptid A plant or animal whose existence has been alleged but not confirmed by mainstream science.

diabolical Having the qualities of a devil; outrageously wicked.

enigmatic Mysterious and difficult to understand; puzzling.

ethereal Having an unusual quality that does not seem to be of this world.

G-man A special agent of the Federal Bureau of Investigation (FBI). The term is probably short for "government man."

high strangeness Inexplicable effects occurring before, during, and after UFO sightings and close encounters.

hypnagogic Of or relating to the state of drowsiness before sleep.

hypnotic regression A technique that uses hypnosis to recover memories that have been stored in the subconscious.

macabre Horrifying and repellent; ghastly.

modus operandi A distinct pattern or mode of operating.

occult Of or relating to supernatural powers or practices.

phantosmia The perception of smell in the absence of physical odors; olfactory hallucination.

poltergeist A ghost or spirit believed to manifest its presence through noises and acts of mischief.

scryer A crystal gazer or seer.

simulacrum (pl. simulacra) A superficial likeness or semblance.

synchronicity The simultaneous occurrence of events that seem to be meaningfully connected but do not have a causal relationship.

ufologist One who studies reports and evidence of UFOs and related phenomena.

For More Information

Center for UFO Studies (CUFOS)
P.O. Box 31335
Chicago, IL 60631
(773) 271-3611
Web site: http://www.cufos.org
CUFOS is an international group of scientists, academics, investigators, and volunteers dedicated to the continuing examination and analysis of the UFO phenomenon.

Encounters: UFO Experience
Broadway at the Beach
1138 Celebrity Circle, Unit 323
Myrtle Beach, SC 29577
(843) 353-0046
Web site: http://ufoexhibition.com

This exhibition focuses on historical and current UFO reports
and alleged alien contacts. Galleries feature topics including unsolved ancient mysteries, military involvement
with UFOs, and pop culture's obsession with aliens and
outer space.

Fortean Times Magazine
International Media Service
3330 Pacific Avenue, Suite 500
Virginia Beach, VA 23451-2983
(800) 428-3003
Web site: http://www.forteantimes.com
Fortean Times has reported on all things unusual for more
than forty years. Covering subjects such as UFOs, conspiracy theories, historical mysteries, and cryptozoology,
it is an entertaining and informative resource for those
interested in strange phenomena.

International UFO Museum and Research Center
114 North Main Street
Roswell, NM 88203
(800) 822-3545
Web site: http://www.roswellufomuseum.com
This museum provides information to the general public on
all aspects of the UFO phenomenon. Museum exhib-
its include information on the Roswell Incident, crop
circles, UFO sightings, Area 51, abductions, and more.

UFO Magazine
P.O. Box 245
Lambertville, NJ 08530

(888) UFO-MAGA [836-6242]

Web site: http://www.ufomag.com

UFO Magazine is a publication for readers with an interest in the paranormal. It reports information about UFO sightings, abductions, conspiracy theories, current research in the field, and new technologies.

Web Sites

Due to the changing nature of Internet links, Rosen Publishing has developed an online list of Web sites related to the subject of this book. This site is updated regularly. Please use this link to access the list:

http://www.rosenlinks.com/OTR/MIB

For Further Reading

Barker, Gray. *Men in Black: The Secret Terror Among Us*. Seattle, WA: Metadisc Books, 2011.

Birnes, William J. *The Everything UFO Book: An Investigation of Sightings, Cover-Ups, and the Quest for Extraterrestrial Life*. Avon, MA: Adams Media, 2012.

Bringle, Jennifer. *Alien Sightings in America* (America's Supernatural Secrets). New York, NY: Rosen Publishing, 2012.

Burgan, Michael. *Searching for UFOs, Aliens, and Men in Black* (Unexplained Phenomena). Mankato, MN: Capstone Press, 2011.

Farndon, John. *Do Not Open: An Encyclopedia of the World's Best-Kept Secrets*. London, UK: DK Publishing, 2010.

Halls, Kelly Milner, and Rick Spears. *Alien Investigation: Searching for the Truth About UFOs and Aliens*. Minneapolis, MN: Millbrook Press, 2012.

Hofer, Jordan. *Saucerville*. Portland, OR: Inkwater Press, 2013.

Keel, John A. *The Mothman Prophecies*. 1st trade pbk ed. New York, NY: Tor, 2013.

Picknett, Lynn. *The Mammoth Book of UFOs*. New York, NY: Constable & Robinson, 2012.

Pilkington, Mark. *Mirage Men: An Adventure into Paranoia, Espionage, Psychological Warfare, and UFOs*. New York, NY: Skyhorse Publishing, 2010.

Pipe, Jim. *Aliens*. New York, NY: Gareth Stevens Publishing, 2013.

Portman, Michael. *Are UFOs Real?* (Space Mysteries). New York, NY: Gareth Stevens Publishing, 2013.

Randle, Kevin D. *Alien Mysteries, Conspiracies, & Cover-Ups*. Canton, MI: Visible Ink, 2013.

Redfern, Nick. *Keep Out! Top Secret Places Governments Don't Want You to Know About*. Pompton Plains, NJ: New Page Books, 2012.

Southwell, David, and Sean Twist. *Unsolved Extraterrestrial Mysteries* (Mysteries and Conspiracies). New York, NY: Rosen Publishing, 2008.

Webb, Stuart. *UFOs* (Paranormal Files). New York, NY: Rosen Publishing, 2013.

Bibliography

"'Aesthetic Prowler' on the loose, Mrs. Kearney and daughter first victims." *Daily Journal-Gazette*. September 2, 1944.

"Albany Rural Cemetery." *www.albanyruralcemetery.org/albrurcem/index.html*.

"Albert Bender and the Three Men in Black." *www.think-aboutit.com/ufo/albert_bender_and_the_three_men_.htm*.

"The Alchemy Web site." *www.levity.com/alchemy/index.html*.

"Alexandra David-Neel Official Web site." *www.alexandra-david-neel.org/index_anim.htm*.

"All About Epilepsy and Seizures." *www.epilepsy.com/Epilepsy/main_epilepsy*, November 2, 2007.

Bajuk, Lidija. "Fairies." *www.leluya.org/mythology/fairies.php*.

Balisunset. "Gray Barker and the *UFO Magazine*: The Saucerian." *http://socyberty.com/paranormal/gray-barker-and-the-ufo-magazine-the-saucerian*, September 9, 2008.

Barker, Gray. *M.I.B.: The Secret Terror Among Us*. Jane Lew, W.V.: New Age Press, 1983.

———. *The Silver Bridge*. Clarksburg, W.V.: Saucerian Books, 1970.

245

————. *They Knew Too Much about Flying Saucers*. Clarksburg, W.V.: Saucerian Press, Inc., 1975.

————. "UFO Creatures on the Prowl." *UFO Report* 3, no. 6 (March 1977).

Barmouth Advertiser. March 30, 1905.

Barrington, Mary Rose. "Kluski." *Psi Researcher*. Winter 1993.

Beckley, Timothy Green. *Curse of the Men in Black*. New Brunswick, N.J.: Global Communications, 2010.

————. *The UFO Silencers*. New Brunswick, N.J.: Inner Light Publications, 1990.

Bender, Albert. *Flying Saucers and the Three Men*. New York: Paperback Library, Inc., 1968.

————. *Space Review* 1, no. 1 (October 1952).

————. *Space Review* 1, no. 4 (October 1953).

————. *Space Review* 2, no. 1 (January 1953).

————. *Space Review* 2, no. 2 (April 1953).

————. *Space Review* 2, no. 3 (July 1953).

Benjamin, R.W. "Tulpa." *www.unknown-creatures.com/tulpa.html*.

Beriah, G. Evans. "Merionethshire Mysteries." *The Occult Review* 1, no. 3 (March 1905).

"Bermuda Triangle Mystery." *www.bermuda-triangle.org*, 2010.

"Board of Investigation into 5 missing TBM airplanes and one PBM airplane convened by Naval Air Advanced Training Command, NAS Jacksonville, Florida 7 December 1945 and related correspondence (Flight 19)." *www.ibiblio.org/hyperwar/USN/rep/Flight19/index.html*.

Boeche, Ray. "Caught in a Web of Deception. Lecture presented at the Gulf Breeze UFO Conference, Gulf Breeze, Florida, February 12, 1994.

Boeche, Raymond W. *Caught in a Web of Deception*. Lincoln, Nebr.: University of Nebraska Press, 1994.

"Boleskine House." *www.thelemapedia.org/index.php/Boleskine_House*, November 21, 2005.

Booth, Martin. *A Magick Life: The Life of Aleister Crowley*. London: Coronet Books, 2000.

Bord, Janet, and Colin Bord. *Alien Animals*. Harrisburg, Pa.: Stackpole Books, 1981.

Brown, Hamish. "What Happened at the Home of Crowley." *www.rinf.com/news/july-05/16.html*, January 24, 2007.

Clark, Jerome. "Men in Black." *Proceedings of the First International UFO Congress*. New York: Warner Books, 1980.

———. "UFO (Unidentified Falling Object) and MIB (Man in Brown)." *UFO Report*. 7, no. 3 (August 1979).

Coleman, Loren. *Mysterious America*. Boston: Faber and Faber, 1983.

Colvin, Andrew B. *The Mothman's Photographer II*. Seattle: Metadisc Books, 2007.

———. *The Mothman's Photographer III*. Seattle: Metadisc Books, 2009.

Cornelius, J. Edward. *Aleister Crowley and the Ouija Board*. Port Townsend, Wash.: Feral House, 2005.

Corrales, Scott. "Sharp Dressed Men: The Men in Black are Back." *Inexplicita: The Journal of Hispanic Ufology* (December 2004).

"The Cosmic Jokers: Dr. Herbert Hopkins MIB Encounter." *http://graylien.110mb.com/hopkins.html*.

Curran, Bob. *Dark Fairies*. Pompton Plains, N.J.: New Page Books, 2010.

Davenport, Elaine, Paul Eddy, and Mark Hurwitz. *The Hughes Papers*. London: Sphere Books, Ltd., 1977.

David-Neel, Alexandra. *Magic and Mystery in Tibet*. New York: Dover Publications, Inc., 1971.

Dinsdale, Tim. *The Leviathans*. Aylesbury, England: Futura Publications, Ltd., 1976.

Downes, Jonathan. *Monster Hunter*. Woolsery, England: CFZ Press, 2004.

Downes, Jonathan, and Nigel Wright. *The Rising of the Moon*. Bangor, Maine: Xiphos Books, 2005.

Drake, Rufus. "Return of the 'Men in Black.'" *UFO Report* 3, no. 4 (October 1976).

Durant, F.C. "Report of Scientific Advisory Panel on Unidentified Flying Objects Convened by Office of Scientific Intelligence, CIA. January 14-18, 1953," *www.cufon.org/cufon/robert.htm*.

Ellis, Bill. *Raising the Devil*. Lexington, Ky.: University of Kentucky Press, 2000.

"Epilepsy, Jacksonian," *www.medterms.com/script/main/art.asp?articlekey=7455*, February 5, 2004.

Evans-Wentz, W.Y. *The Fairy-Faith in Celtic Countries*. Pompton Plains, N.J.: New Page Books, 2004.

Federal Bureau of Investigation files on Arnold, Kenneth, 1947.

Federal Bureau of Investigation files on Barker, Gray, November 1958.

Federal Bureau of Investigation files on Bender, Albert, February–October 1954.

Federal Bureau of Investigation files on Bender, Albert, November 1958.

Federal Bureau of Investigation files on Perry, Joseph, 1960.

Federal Bureau of Investigation files on UFO sightings over Washington, D.C., July 1952.

Freeman, Richard. *Dragons: More Than a Myth?* Woolsery, England: CFZ Press, 2005.

Fuller, John G. *The Interrupted Journey*. New York: Dial Press, 1966.

Gibbons, Gavin. *By Space Ship to the Moon*. London: Blackwell Publishers, 1958.

Goerman, Robert A. "The Men in Black Exist!" *Official UFO* (March 1977).

Goldberg, Dr. Bruce. "Time Travelers I Have Met." *www
.drbrucegoldberg.com/TimeTravelers2.htm*.

Greenberg, Paul. "Sightings: Men in Black." *www.ufoevidence
.org/documents/doc1697.htm*.

Greenfield, Allen H. *Secret Cypher of the UFOnauts*. Lilburn,
Ga.: Illuminet Press, 1994.

———. *Secret Rituals of the Men in Black*. Raleigh, N.C.: Lulu,
2005.

"The Grove Park Inn's Pink Lady." *http://shadowboxent.brinkster
.net/lemurpinklady.html*.

Hall, Mark A. *Thunderbirds*. New York: Paraview Press, 2004.

Harmsworth, A.J. "Loch Ness Information Web site." *www
.loch-ness.org*, 2010.

Hansen, George P. *The Trickster and the Paranormal*.
Philadelphia: Xlibris, 2001.

Harney, John. "Should 'Men in Black' reports be taken seriously?"
Merseyside UFO Bulletin 1, no. 5 (September–October
1968).

Holiday, F.W. *The Dragon and the Disc*. Aylesbury, England:
Futura Publications, Ltd., 1974.

———. "Exorcism and UFO Landing at Loch Ness." *Flying
Saucer Review* 19, no. 5 (September–October 1973).

———. *The Great Orm of Loch Ness*. London: Faber & Faber,
Ltd., 1968.

Holiday, Ted. *The Goblin Universe*. St. Paul, Minn.: Llewellyn
Publications, 1986.

Hough, Peter. "The Green Alien of Ilkley Moor." *Fate* (March
1999).

Hynek, Dr. J. Allen. *The Hynek UFO Report*. London: Sphere
Books, Ltd., 1978.

———. *The UFO Experience*. London: Corgi, 1979.

"The Ilkley Moor Encounter of the Third Kind." *www.ufologie
.net/htm/ilkleymoor.htm*, March 7, 2002.

Imbrogno, Philip J., and Rosemary Ellen Guiley. *The Vengeful Djinn*. St. Paul, Minn.: Llewellyn Publications, 2011.

"Impersonations of Air Force Officers." Department of the Air Force, March 1, 1967.

Kaczynski, Richard. *Perdurabo: The Life of Aleister Crowley*. Las Vegas, Nev.: New Falcon Publications, 2002.

Kaku, Michio. *Physics of the Impossible*. New York: Anchor Books, 2009.

Keel, John A. *The Fickle Finger of Fate*. Greenwich, Conn.: Fawcett Publications, Inc., 1966.

———. *Jadoo*. New York: J. Messner, 1957.

———. *The Mothman Prophecies*. New York: Tor, 1991.

———. "Mysterious Voices from Outer Space." *UFO Report* 2, no. 6 (Winter 1975).

———. *Our Haunted Planet*. London: Futura Publications Ltd., 1971.

———. *UFOs: Operation Trojan Horse*. London: Souvenir Press, Ltd., 1971.

———. *Visitors from Space*. St. Albans, UK: Panther Books, Ltd., 1976.

Keith, Jim. *Casebook of the Men in Black*. Lilburn, Ga.: IllumiNet Press, 1997.

Kimball, Paul, and Red Star Films. "The Island of Blood." *www.youtube.com/watch?v=wbRZLtei_4o*, February 1, 2010.

Kincaid, Brad. "Tulpas: Creating a Being Through Thoughts Alone." *www.helium.com/items/538207-tulpas-creating-a-being-through-thoughts-alone*, 2010.

Kithra. "The Cumberland Spaceman and the Ilkley Moor Alien." *http://kithraskrystalkave.org.uk/cumberlandspaceman.htm*, Spring 2008.

"Legend of Nessie." *www.nessie.co.uk*, November 29, 2010.

Lewis, David Allen, and Robert Shreckhise. *UFO: End-Time Delusion*. Green Forest, Ark: New Leaf Press, 1991.

Mality, Dr. Abner. "The Wormwood Files: The Darkest Strangers." *www.wormwoodchronicles.com/wormwood-files/men-in-black*.

Maruna, Scott. *The Mad Gasser of Mattoon*. Jacksonville, Fla.: Swamp Gas Book Company, 2007.

Mayo Clinic Staff. "Hypochondria." *www.mayoclinic.com/health/hypochondria/DS00841*, November 23, 2010.

———. "Migraine." *www.mayoclinic.com/health/migraine-headache/DS00120*, June 6, 2009.

"The Mediumship of Franek Kluski." *www.fortunecity.com/roswell/seance/78/kl.htm*.

Melnick, Monte A., and Frank Meyer. *On the Road With the Ramones*. London: Sanctuary Publishing Ltd., 2003.

"Men in Black." *www.imdb.com/title/tt0119654*.

"Men in Black Facts." *www.paranormalnewscentral.com/conspiracies/articles/235-men-in-black-facts*.

Moseley, James W., and Karl T. Pflock. *Shockingly Close to the Truth*. Amherst, N.Y.: Prometheus Books, 2002.

Moseley, James W. *Saucer News*, no. 29 (November 1967).

Murch, Robert. "The Official Web site of William Fuld." *www.williamfuld.com*, 2007.

Murray, Frank. "Saga of the Men in Black." *Beyond Reality*, no. 18 (January 1976).

"The Museum of Talking Boards." *www.museumoftalkingboards.com/WebOuija.html*, 2010.

"The Mysterious Thunderbird Photo." *www.prairieghosts.com/tbirdaz.html*, 2008.

"Mystery Men Plague UFO Witnesses." *UFO Report*. Franklin Park, Ill.: Modern People Productions, Inc., 1975.

National Archive file reference number on Anne Henson's 1962 UFO encounter: AIR/ 2/16918.

National Institute of Mental Health. "Obsessive Compulsive Disorder, OCD." *www.nimh.nih.gov/health/topics/obsessive-compulsive-disorder-ocd/index.shtml*.

"National Investigations Committee on Aerial Phenomena." *www.nicap.org*, December 15, 1997.

Newbern, Kathy M., and Fletcher. "J.S., Lady in Pink: Grove Park Inn's Out-of-this-World Guest." *www.southerntravelnews .com/NewsRelease.aspx?NewsId=132*, March 5, 2007.

Newman, F.B. "Who are the 'Men in Black?'" *UFO Magazine*, no. 1 (March 1978).

O'Brien, Christopher. *Enter the Valley*. New York: St. Martin's Press, 1999.

———. *The Mysterious Valley*. New York: St. Martin's Press, 1996.

———. *Stalking the Tricksters*. Kempton, Ill.: Adventures Unlimited Press, 2009.

"Poltergeist." *www.themystica.com/mystica/articles/p/poltergeist.html*.

Radin, Paul. *The Trickster: A Study in American Indian Mythology*. New York: Philosophical Library, 1956.

Randles, Jenny. *MIB: Investigating the Truth Behind the Men in Black Phenomenon*. London: Piatkus, 1997.

Redfern, Nick. *Contactees*. Pompton Plains, N.J.: New Page Books, 2009.

———. *Cosmic Crashes*. London: Simon & Schuster, 1999.

———. *A Covert Agenda*. London: Simon & Schuster, 1997.

———. *The FBI Files*. London: Simon & Schuster, 1998.

———. *Final Events*. New York: Anomalist Books, 2010.

———. *Memoirs of a Monster Hunter*. Pompton Plains, N.J.: New Page Books, 2007.

———. *On the Trail of the Saucer Spies*. New York: Anomalist Books, 2006.

Roberts, Andy. *UFO Down?* Woolsery, England: Fortean Words, 2010.

Rojcewicz, Peter M. "The 'Men in Black' Experience and Tradition: Analogues with the Traditional Devil Hypothesis." *The Journal of American Folklore* 100, no. 396 (April–June 1987).

Roll, William G. *The Poltergeist*. New York: New American Library, 1972.

———. *Unleashed*. New York: Paraview-Pocket, 2004.

"Saucers and Citizens." *UFO Magazine*, no. 4 (December 1978).

Schwarz, Berthold Eric. *UFO Dynamics*. Moore Haven, Fla.: Rainbow Books, 1983.

Scot, Reginald. *The Discoverie of Witchcraft*. New York: Dover Publications, 1972.

Scottish Tourist Board. "Loch Ness Center and Exhibition." *www.lochness.com*, 2006.

Seifried, Richard D. "Those Mysterious MIBs." *Oklahoma MUFONEWS* (April 1993).

Serendip. "Hypnagogia: A Bridge to Other Realities." *http://serendip.brynmawr.edu/exchange/node/1800*, January 9, 2008.

Sergent, Jr., Donnie, and Jeff Wamsley. *Mothman: The Facts Behind the Legend*. Self-published via Mark S. Phillips Publishing, Proctorville, Ohio, 2001.

Sherwood, John C. "Gray Barker: My Friend, the Myth-Maker." *Skeptical Inquirer* 23 (May–June 1998).

Sideshow's Library. "Enema Bandit." *http://haycriminal.blogspot.com/2009/02/enema-bandit.html*, February 7, 2009.

Skinner, Doug. "John A. Keel: A Brief Biography." *www.johnkeel.com/?page_id=21*, November 29, 2010.

Smith, Russell James. *Tulpa*. Self-published via iUniverse, Inc., Bloomington, Ind., 2003.

Starkey, Marion L. *The Devil in Massachusetts*. New York: Anchor Books, 1949.

Steiger, Brad. *Mysteries of Space and Time*. New York: Dell, 1977.

———. *Revelation: The Divine Fire*. Upper Saddle River, N.J.: Prentice Hall, 1973.

———. "Three Tricksters in Black." *Saga's UFO Report* (Winter 1974).

Steinmeyer, Jim. *Charles Fort: The Man Who Invented the Supernatural*. New York: Penguin Group, 2008.

Sutin, Lawrence. *Do What Thou Wilt: A Life of Aleister Crowley*. London: Pindar Press, 2000.

Symonds, John. *The Beast 666: The Life of Aleister Crowley*. New York: St. Martin's Press, 1997.

"Tulpa Creation." *www.tulpa.com/explain/tulpaexplain.html*.

Turner, Karla. *Into the Fringe*. New York: Berkley Books, 1992.

"UFO link with pony deaths." *Daily News*. Durban, South Africa, July 15, 1977.

Vallee, Jacques. *Messengers of Deception*. Brisbane, Australia: Daily Grail Publishing, 2008.

———. *Passport to Magonia*. London: Neville Spearman, 1970.

Wall, James Charles. *Devils: Their Origins and History*. Plymouth, UK: William Brendon & Sons, 1904.

Wallace, Chevon. "Albert Bender and the M.I.B. Mystery." *http://bridgeport.ct.schoolwebpages.com/education/components/scrapbook/default.php?sectiondetailid=25228*, November 29, 2010.

Walsh, Daev. "Walking the Dead: Charles Fort's Grave—Albany, New York." *http://blather.net/blather/2007/05/charles_fort_grave_albany_new_york.html*, May 10, 2007.

Wamsley, Jeff. *Mothman: Behind the Red Eyes*. Point Pleasant, W.V.: Mothman Press, 2005.

———. "The Mothman Lives." *www.mothmanlives.com*, 2008.

Warren, Larry, and Peter Robbins. *Left at East Gate*. New York: Cosimo, 2005.

Weil, Dr. Andrew. "Phantosmia: Smelling Smoke all the Time?" *www.drweil.com/drw/u/QAA400682/Phantosmia-Smelling-Smoke-All-the-Time.html*, February 5, 2010.

Weldon, John, and Zolam Levitt. *UFOs: What on Earth is Happening?* Irvine, Calif.: Harvest House Publishers, 1975.

Wheless, Lieutenant General Hewitt T. U.S. Air Force memorandum. March 1, 1967.

"Whispers from Space." *http://whispersfromspace.com*, 1995.

Wilhelm, Allan R. "Grand Blanc Man Photographs Saucer." *Flint Journal* (March 28, 1960).

Wilkins, Harold T. *Flying Saucers on the Attack*. New York: Ace Books, Inc., 1954.

———. *Flying Saucers Uncensored*. New York: The Citadel Press, 1955.

Williamson, George Hunt. *Secret Places of the Lion*. London: Neville Spearman, 1969.

Witchell, Nicholas. *The Loch Ness Story*. London: Corgi Books, 1982.

Worley, Don. "The Winged Lady in Black." *Flying Saucer Review*, *Case Histories*, no. 10 (June 1972).

Author Interviews and Correspondence

Beckley, Timothy Green, interview with, September 21, 2010.

Bennett, Colin, interview with, October 9, 2010.

Bishop, Greg, interview with, September 23, 2010.

Boeche, Ray, interview with, September 24, 2010.

Bott, Irene, interview with, November 18, 1996.

Clark, Jerome, interview with, October 20, 2010.

Coleman, Loren, statement given from, November 29, 2010.

Cunningham, Claudia, interview with, September 16, 2010.

"Doctor" (anonymous), interview with, March 1, 1998.

Greenfield, Allen, interview with, October 6, 2010.

Hanks, Micah, interview with, September 8, 2010.

Helen, interview with, May 12, 1994.

Henson, Anne, interview with, February 2, 1998.

Jones, Marie, interview with, September 9, 2010.

Lee, Regan, e-mail to, November 10, 2010.

Lee, Regan, e-mail from, November 15, 2010.

Lee, Regan, interview with, September 29, 2010.

Meindel, Raven, interview with, September 4, 2010.

Moseley, Jim, interview with, September 13, 2010.

O'Brien, Chris, interview with, October 4, 2010.

Perks, Colin, interview with, June 12, 2001.

Pope, Nick, interview with, March 29, 1994.

Steiger, Brad, interview with, September 14, 2010.

Warren, Joshua P., interview with, October 6, 2010.

Index

About the Author

Nick Redfern works full-time as an author, lecturer, and journalist. He writes about a wide range of unsolved mysteries, including Bigfoot, UFOs, the Loch Ness Monster, alien encounters, and government conspiracies. He writes regularly for *UFO Magazine*, *Fate*, *TAPS Paramagazine*, and *Fortean Times*. His previous books include *The NASA Conspiracies*, *Contactees*, and *Memoirs of a Monster Hunter*. Redfern has appeared on numerous television shows, including VH1's *Legend Hunters*, the BBC's *Out of this World*, History Channel's *Monster Quest* and *UFO Hunters*, National Geographic Channel's *Paranatural*, and SyFy Channel's *Proof Positive*. He is co-host, with Raven Meindel, of the popular weekly radio show, *Exploring All Realms*. Nick Redfern lives in Arlington, Texas, with his wife, Dana, and can be contacted at nickredfern.com.